What people are saying...

"Allison's book should never leave your sight. It contains a clear path for living your dream and getting more out of life. Here is your chance to stop dreaming about it once and for all and start making something great happen in your life and work. It is your desktop and bedside table companion for life!"

MARK LeBLANC, author of *Growing Your Business!*, president of Small Business Success, past president, National Speakers Association

"Allison Maslan bares her soul in this authentic book about living passionately and fully from the inside out. In Blast Off! she skillfully weaves the power of divine energy and the soul's purpose with nuts and bolts strategy and raw determination. The result is mesmerizing. After reading this book, you will not only know for certain that you can achieve your heart's desire, you will be equipped with the tools make it happen. She is brilliant at teaching others to tap into the deepest part of themselves and then helping them create their individual formula for success. I highly recommend this book."

ERNEST D. CHU, author of *Soul Currency,* spiritual community leader, and counselor

"Allison Maslan is amazing. My dreams have come true after working closely with her program. Blast Off! is completely unique and led me to my road of success. Years of dreaming are now manifesting as a speaker and writer due solely to her program. Thank you, Allison!"

JEANNE STRYKER, M.D.

"Allison Maslan has given us a book that not only inspires us but also shows us the path for our newfound passion to follow. This is a rare self-help tutorial with a road map. Ms. Maslan has ingeniously shed the light on 'how to do it' after she has delivered the 'what to do.' The ingredients for success are motivation, inspiration, and passion. This is the book that makes it clear how to put them to use."

JOE HARPER, president of Del Mar Thoroughbred Club and Racetrack

"Blast Off! is an entertaining guidebook that reveals how to make your dreams become a reality—complete with your own personal flight plan, prelaunch check list, and enough fuel to reach the stratosphere in personal achievement. Allison shows that harnessing your passion and fulfilling your soul's goals 'ain't rocket science!' She's helped countless others before, and now Blast Off! can prepare you to lift off on your own mission of sky-high success."

C. RUSSELL BRUMFIELD, bestselling author of *Whiff!*

"How sweet is this! A beautifully crafted book, jam-pack full of bright wisdom, heartwarming stories, and brilliant ideas. Let it be your personal coach and you cannot go wrong. It will guide, advise, encourage, and even cheer you on at each and every step of your way, as you craft a vision, breathe life into your dreams, and make them come true."

MIRANDA CASTRO, FSHOM, CCH, homeopath and author, *The Complete Homeopathy Handbook; Homeopathy for Pregnancy, Birth, and Your Baby's First Years;* and *A Homeopathic Guide to Stress*

"*This is a wonderful book of great assistance to anyone seeking the next step in life's journey. It is a user manual to manifesting one's dreams. Often in my practice, my patients who get well will ask, 'Now what?' Allison's book provides the answer.*"

TODD ROWE M.D., M.D. (H), CCH, DHT, president of The American Medical College of Homeopathy and author, *Homeopathic Methodology* and *The Homeopathic Journey*

"*In* Blast Off! *Allison Maslan provides us with the keys to manifesting what in the yogic tradition are called the Four Fruits of Life—dharma (the true path), artha (prosperity), kama (love), and moksha (freedom). Allison shares generously from her life experiences and humorously recounts how from them she learned to discover her true calling, find the man of her dreams, build a successful business, face her fears, and have a lot of fun along the way. Allison's gift is to present universal and eternal principles in a way that is easy to understand and apply.*"

TIM MILLER, owner/director, Ashtanga Yoga Center (Encinitas, California) The first American certified to teach by Pattabhi Jois at the Ashtanga Yoga Research Institute in Mysore, India

"*In* Blast Off! *Allison shares the story of her personal journey from despair to triumph. It's an insightful and engaging book, filled with specific actions you can take right now. It will inspire you to transform your own life from so-so to supersonic, just like Allison did. What a great read!*"

SARAH Z. SLEEPER, award-winning journalist and past vice-president of The National Writers Union

"*Allison Maslan's powerful book,* Blast Off! *gives the most direct path in inventing the career and personal life of your dreams. Her easy-to-follow flight plan is a profound mix of inspiration, passion, and success in the real world.*"

DIGBY DIEHL, *New York Times* and *London Times* bestselling author of over 30 books, including *Million Dollar Mermaid, Remembering Grace*, literary correspondent for ABC-TV's "Good Morning America," and founding editor of *The Los Angeles Times Book Review*

"*If you heard that a simple, fun-to-read book could assist you in achieving your dreams and overcoming the roadblocks that have stood in your way, wouldn't you rush out to see what all the fuss was about? I did... and I couldn't be happier with Allison's clear life dictates and her passionate encouragement, which helped propel me forward to realize my goals.*"

MATTHEW TILKER, president of Mistral and screenwriter

BLAST OFF!

The Surefire
Success Plan to
Launch Your Dreams
into Reality

WORKBOOK

Allison Maslan, HHP, CCH

NEW YORK

Blast Off!
The Surefire Success Plan to Launch Your Dreams into Reality
WORKBOOK
Allison Maslan, HHP, CCH

ISBN 978-1-60037-697-9 (paperback)
Library of Congress 2009932357

Published by:
MORGAN · JAMES
THE ENTREPRENEURIAL PUBLISHER ™
www.morganjamespublishing.com

Morgan James Publishing
1225 Franklin Ave. Ste 325
Garden City, NY 11530-1693
Toll Free 800-485-4943
www.MorganJamesPublishing.com

*Blast Off! Life Coaching*SM is a trademark of Allison Maslan.

*Blast Off! The Surefire Success Plan to Launch Your Dreams into Reality*SM is a trademark of Allison Maslan, and it is referred to in this book as The *Blast Off! Program.*

Edited by Sarah Z. Sleeper and Robin Quinn
Book cover and interior designed by Peri Poloni-Gabriel, Knockout Design
Cover photo and author photo by Leslie Bohm
Illustrations by Mia Fortescue

BLASTATION
Interactive Life Coaching Software

Blastation is a completely unique interactive life-coaching software program that can be utilized to work the *Blast Off! Program*. I developed *Blastation* when I was unable to find an adequate goal-setting software to use with my *Blast Off! Life Coaching* clients. It's a lively software that helps keep you organized, optimistic and inspired so you can make your dream life a reality.

Blastation is like no other goal-setting/life-planning software. It's Web-based like Yahoo or Google, so it is at your disposal anywhere that you can get Internet access. This is a one-of-a-kind software that enables you to clarify and attain your large and small life dreams and visions. Then *Blastation* helps you break these goals down into easy-to-follow incremental steps that you are more likely to achieve. These steps are then posted on your personalized online *Blastation Calendar* to keep your personal and professional life organized. (In fact, you can use *Blastation* to send e-mails and host your online address book, too.) *Blastation* is the catalyst to envision your dreams, then strategize to make them happen.

> "Blastation is your virtual space to dream, design, envision and implement the life you've always wanted."
>
> ~Allison Maslan

As you work with the *Blast Off! Program*, it's perfectly fine to work strictly with the *Blast Off!* book and the *Blast Off! Workbook*. However, it is highly recommended that you also consider accessing the tools contained in the *Blastation* program for added reinforcement. Visit the website, www.InteractiveLifeCoach.com for a test drive and more information.

Awaken the dormant spark
that lights the pathway to your soul.
Then watch your passion burn
like wildfire.

~Allison Maslan

Table of Contents

Life is a succession of moments...
to live each one is to succeed.

~Corita Kent,
Artist and educator
(1918-1986)

As time passes, and you soar along your personal *Blast Off! Path*, you will encounter many opportunities for more dreams and *Big Picture Visions*. Please reuse the practices and tools described in this workbook for each and every desired aspiration. The tools and practices will help you gain clarity and focus for your direction, and push you past any unexpected bumps in the road. And most of all, they will facilitate the launch of your *Supersonic* dreams into reality!

Here's a recap on how to use the basic *Blast Off! Tools*:

First, write a *Big Picture Vision* for each area in which you want to create change or wish to move to higher levels of success and prosperity. Each *Big Picture Vision* should be the ultimate, most beautiful and satisfying end-result you could ever imagine. You can create these *Big Picture Visions* on copies of the *Big Picture Vision Board* form or in the *Blastation* software.

Then you break down each *Big Picture Vision* into the crucial *Mile Steps*—these are BIG steps needed to make that vision a reality. Jot down your *Miles Steps* on the *Mile Steps Spreadsheet* or input them into the *Blastation* software.

Next, it's time to break down the *Miles Steps* into small daily *Mini Feats*—the valued activities or tasks that move you forward to the accomplishment of a *Mile Step*. Mini Feats only take a minimum of five minutes each to complete, but you may be so motivated that you will do the Feat for a longer time. You can create *Mini Feats* on the *Mile Steps Spreadsheet* or type them into the *Blastation* software.

It's best to chart out the timing of your *Mini Feats* each week. Sunday is a good day to plan this out. That way, you'll start your week on an upswing. Set a day and time on the *Mini Feat Calendar* or in the *Blastation* software.

(Note: All of these forms can be found in the back of the workbook.)

And last but not least, don't forget to begin each day with your powerful *Sun-Up Script* and *Rocket Words*. These tools will enable you to blast off daily in an inspired state with a clear head and heart.

Here's to your *Blast Off!*

How to Use the
Blast Off! Workbook

This workbook is an accompaniment to the winning book, *Blast Off! The Surefire Success Plan to Launch Your Dreams into Reality*. It provides you with the creative space to work through the many powerful practices. As a companion book, the workbook functions as an extension of the main book—*Blast Off!*—rather than a standalone activity book, because it doesn't contain the philosophy or background behind the core of the *Blast Off! Program*. All the information you need to fully succeed with my program is in the main book, *Blast Off!*

I recommend reading from the beginning of the main book—*Blast Off!*—up through the Introduction and continuing to where the first *Blast Off! Practice* (Design Your Own *Personal Life Path*) begins in Chapter One. Then come to the workbook to work with that practice. Afterwards, continue to read through Chapter One in the main book, and on through the subsequent chapters, utilizing the companion *Blast Off! Workbook* to process and work with the remaining practices that you come across.

Launchtime Practices

Each of the chapters ahead features the topic-related *Launchtime Practices* from *Blast Off!* These are compelling exercises designed to help you develop and actualize your success. As you work through the many challenging, yet insightful exercises, you may choose to do them on your own, or with a partner or group. The *Blastation Interactive Life Coaching Software* also gives you the opportunity to work through select exercises from the chapters.

The exercises can be done sequentially in every chapter as you read through *Blast Off!* or you may want to start with the ones in each chapter that you resonate with the most. If you take the second approach,

> ## "The secret of success is consistency to purpose."
>
> *~Benjamin Disraeli,*
> *British Prime Minister,*
> *novelist, essayist*
> *(1804-1881)*

go back later and perform any exercises to which you may have felt resistant. We often resist what we need most!

Many people have been surprised, even shocked, to see what is revealed in this creative process. They are even further amazed at how much passion is accessed and how many dreams are realized from working through the practices and utilizing the tools I've incorporated into the *Blast Off! Program*.

Your Daily Launch Tools

There are a few **Daily Launch Tools** that you'll use throughout the *Blast Off! Program*, and it is my hope that you'll continue to use them once you've completed it. They are separate support systems from the *Launchtime Practices* and will be used to design, develop and direct you to your *Blast Off!* life.

I've found that people are more successful in actualizing their dreams and goals when they are operating within a certain routine or structure. This doesn't mean that your life must be predictable or stifling. *Quite the opposite.* This structure will represent a source of power and strength that you may draw from, while offering stability to ground you when fear or uncertainty arise. Think of them as your fear fighters. These *Daily Launch Tools* will help create a foundation for attaining and maintaining your success.

> **Note:** *Forms for the* Big Picture Vision *and* Weekly Flight Assessments *(two of the three* Daily Launch Tools *described below) can be found in the back of this book and may be photocopied for use. You can also work with these two tools in the Blastation software, the powerful interactive life-coaching program described earlier. (Visit www.InteractiveLifeCoach.com to learn more.)*

Sun-Up Scripts

The first tool is called the *Sun-Up Script*. This is a free-association writing exercise to assist you in releasing the negative thought process, or any gunk in your brain that you may be starting your day with. It's also a modality to explore your hidden talents, inspiring thoughts, creative artistry and ingenious ideas.

This is how it works. I recommend using a separate journal devoted solely to your *Sun-Up Scripts*. Alternatively, the scripts can be created right in the *Blastation* software at www.InteractiveLifeCoach.com. The *Blast Off! Workbook* does not have space for your *Sun-Up Scripts,* and its pages are largely focused on the *Launchtime Practices*.

At the top of a blank page, you'll write the first word or statement that comes to your mind. This is your **theme word or phrase.** Then write as much as you need to about that word or statement and whatever comes up spontaneously about it. You're not allowed to analyze or judge your thoughts, just spill out all the beauty or ugliness right onto the page or into the computer. Release every bit of pent-up energy or feelings from your brain, your heart, your gut and your spirit through your pen to the paper or through your fingers to the computer.

When you feel that you've fully addressed the word or phrase, after about a page or more of free association scribbling or typing, ask yourself if you feel complete. Have your feelings about this theme word or phrase changed at all? I liken this process to a good cry or scream. The *Sun-Up Scripts* are a vehicle to release an incredible amount of negative energy, or a catalyst to pump up an already positive mindset. This passionate writing may offer words or insight that you had not considered. It can offer effective solace and solutions to get you back on track or move you to the next level.

Each morning's *Sun-Up Script* can have up to three theme words or phrases.

Example

Theme Word: *Overwhelmed*

I have so much work to do this week! I am not sure how everything is going to get done. Why do I pile so much onto myself? Errrrggghhhh!

I am so exhausted and I have no help. I just want to crawl back in bed. I have so much I want to do, but I have no time. When is it ever going to be my time? I am so sick of doing for everyone else and I have no energy left for me. So why do I keep saying "yes" when I really want to say "no?!" I am going to practice saying "no" every day this week and see how it feels. The thought of it seems so freeing. No No No No No No No!!! I feel soooo much better!

Then finish up the *Sun-Up Script* with your **Rocket Words** for the day, a summarizing sentence with a positive twist. This sentence will be your mantra, a phrase of strength for this day, which will assist in flip-switching any negative attitudes or vibes to positive energetic frequencies. (If your theme words or phrases were already positive, your *Rocket Words* will provide added support to keep you in this positive flow.) In the case of the writer of the Overwhelmed *Sun-Up Script* above, the *Rocket Words* for the day might be:

> *"I feel ready and able to take on whatever today brings."*

Post your *Rocket Words* wherever your attention may be focused in your environment—on your bathroom mirror, the fridge, on your computer desktop on *Blastation* software. Every time you catch a glimpse of your *Rocket Words for the Day*, they will remind you to stay tuned to this high frequency. And the more time you spend in this upbeat easy flow, the more likely your day will grace you with energy, productivity and fun.

> "Without continual growth and progress, words like improvement, achievement and success have no meaning."
>
> *~Benjamin Franklin, Author, printer, statesman and inventor (1706-1790)*

Mini Feats

The second tool is called your **Mini Feats**. These are successive small accomplishments that add up to greater achievements. The steps involve courage, strength and commitment. They are action steps in small increments that require only five minutes to do.

Sometimes our goals can feel so huge and daunting. We often make lists with the best intentions of accomplishing everything on them. And then, because life takes over, we are not able to get the tasks done. We keep transferring those tasks to the next day or the next week. This only adds feelings of frustration and self-criticism to our already full plate.

Fractioning a project into five-minute increments makes it easy and fun. And surprisingly, you will finish the task and reach your goal much faster than you would expect. You can do just about anything for five minutes! And often, once you get started, you will be even more motivated to finish your task and may give it more time. But, remember, you are only required to spend five minutes on each *Mini Feat.*

You may be thinking, "How much progress can be made in five minutes?" Well, if you do three five-minute valued tasks each day, that will be twenty-one tasks completed by the week's end! The secret is to spend less time doubting, and more time doing.

Write down your *Mini Feats* with the date and time you are committing to take action. For this effort, you might use the form in the back of this book (the *Mini Feat Calendar*), a day-planner booklet, or the weekly or monthly calendar provided in the *Blastation* program.

For instance, if you keep procrastinating paying your bills, then you might set up your *Mini Feats* for the week like this:

Mini-Feats for
"Creating a Better System for Paying Bills"

Tuesday at 6:30 PM : *Put all bills together with the envelopes, stamps, checkbook and calculator.*

Wednesday at 8:00 PM : *Take bills out of the envelopes, and apply stamps and return address stickers on the return envelopes.*

Thursday at 7:00 PM : *Write checks and then stuff and seal envelopes.*

Friday at 8:00 AM : *Balance my check register and mail the bills!*

If cleaning and organizing your office are overwhelming tasks, try this:

> **Mini Feats for
> "Keeping a Cleaner and More Organized Desk Area"**
>
> **Monday at 10:00 AM:** *Clear off top of desk for five minutes.*
>
> **Tuesday at noon:** *Clear out the top right drawer.*
>
> **Wednesday at 7:30 PM:** *File papers that are on the desk.*
>
> **Thursday at 7:30 AM:** *Clear out top left drawer.*
>
> *...and so on.*

If finding a new career is your *Big Picture Vision*—these are your large goals for specific areas, explained a bit later in this workbook—your *Mini Feats* schedule might be:

> **Mini Feats for
> "Finding a New Career"**
>
> **Monday at 7:00 AM:** *Spend five minutes doing Google searches on career ideas. (Save your findings to read through later.)*
>
> **Tuesday at 10:00 PM:** *Research local business-networking activities around town, via the Internet or local newspapers.*
>
> **Wednesday at 9:30 AM:** *Make call to sign up for networking meeting.*
>
> **Thursday at 11:30 AM:** *Make call to arrange lunch meeting with recent acquaintance to find out more about their career and possible helpful connections.*

By Thursday of the first week, you'll already be making terrific progress!

The *Blast Off! Program* asks that you perform a minimum of three *Mini Feats* per day. They can be from any area of your life that you are working on, or relate to any goals you've set. They need to be three valued activities that will assist you in working toward your objectives or your *Big Picture Vision*. So feeding the fish and watching your favorite reality TV show doesn't count.

Once you have developed two *Long-Range Launch Tools*—the *Big Picture Visions* and *Mile Steps,* explanations to follow—you will be able to map out the *Mini Feats* needed to reach your longer term goals.

> "Everything that is done in the world is done by hope."
>
> ~Martin Luther, German monk, theologian and church reformer (1483-1546)

You should throughtfully write out your *Mini Feats* the night or the week before you plan to do them. Sunday is a good day to plan your week. This way, you'll hit the ground running Monday morning. When you write down your *Mini Feats,* you are also directing your intentions out into the Universe about what you want your days to entail. The energy will already be at work—even while you're sleeping—helping to create the dreams you plan to achieve. (Again, a helpful form for this purpose—the *Mini Feat Calendar*—can be found in the back of this workbook.)

Weekly Flight Assessments

The third tool is called the *Weekly Flight Assessment,* which helps you evaluate and track your weekly progress, gains and roadblocks. This is a quick way to assess your week, keep yourself on track, and see areas you may need to work on. Make a commitment to complete the *Weekly Flight Assessment Log* every week, using a copy of the form from the back of this book.

Over the next several weeks, it will be fun to look back on your earlier *Weekly Flight Assessments* to see just how much progress you've made and how much closer you are to reaching your *Big Picture Vision.* For a further guarantee that you'll keep this promise to yourself, make it a habit to fax or e-mail your *Weekly Flight Assessment Logs* to a supportive friend, co-worker or a member of your *Blast Off! Group.* This practice will help you stay on track with your goals and be accountable to your commitments. It's kind of like weighing in at Weight Watchers. If you know that you're going to be accountable for your diet goals, you're more likely to skip the potatoes and choose extra broccoli instead.

The Daily Launch Tools Checklist

Here are brief explanations of the three *Daily Launch Tools*—the *Sun-Up Scripts, Mini Feats* and *Weekly Flight Assessments*—along with instructions for working them into your schedule.

★ Your personal **Sun-Up Script** will preferably be worked on each morning to get your juices flowing. It's a great way to get your day going in the right state of mind. However, if mornings are not possible, find a fifteen-minute window within each day or evening to write, release and shift any lingering negativity, or to reinforce your already positive perspective.

★ Schedule at least three **Mini Feats** each day to help yourself attain your goals. It may be challenging at first to stay on track with them, yet I assure you that if you utilize them as your new healthy habit, it will be much, much easier to reach your goals. (There are examples of subject-specific *Mini Feats* at the end of each chapter of the workbook on the *Blast Off! Daily Launch Tools* page.)

★ Then complete each week with your **Weekly Flight Assessment** to keep yourself accountable and focused on your goals. Keep the process flowing to reach your *Supersonic gear* where you can say, "This is the Life of My Dreams that I have created and I am loving it!"

Long-Range Launch Tools

Your *Long-Range Launch Tools* will be used to create your *Big Picture Vision*—your goals and dreams. The two long-range tools that I developed—the *Big Picture Vision* and the *Mile Steps*—are extremely effective for the development of your dream career, dream relationship, and every other aspect of your life. They will also help you keep everything straight in your mind, so you can follow through with thoughtful and organized actions. The result? You'll be able to take the most direct route to fulfilling your desires.

Big Picture Vision

Your *Big Picture Vision* is the pot of gold at the end of your rainbow, and this tool can help you determine your desired goals in life. Your *Big Picture Vision* should be the ultimate, most beautiful and satisfying end-result you could ever imagine for each life area. By defining and illustrating your *Big Picture Visions* through images, text or illustration, you will be creating destinations.

> "Dreams are necessary to life."
>
> ~Anais Nin, Cuban-French author known for her best-selling journals (1903-1977)

When you have a destination, even if you're not quite sure how to get there, you can experience some peace in knowing that you're not wandering aimlessly. Why? Because you now have a plan. This knowledge of your end-result will help you focus and target your energy in a clearer, more precise manner. Even if your *Big Picture Vision* is a gigantic undertaking, and it will take months or even years to create, having an illustration and description of your desired destination helps bring it to life. This process will make your large goals much more tangible, much easier to grasp, and that much closer to becoming a reality.

For instance, if one of your *Big Picture Visions* is to redesign a room in your home, you could draw it on a big piece of paper. You would imagine and draw what you want the furniture to look like. You'd position the fixtures where you want them, etc. Crayons or paint can be used to bring your *Big Picture Vision* to life. (It doesn't matter if you're not an artist. No one is critiquing this effort, and the picture is just be for you.)

You could also describe your *Big Picture Vision* in writing. This would be a first-person story in the present tense about what it is like to live your vision. Written *Big Picture Visions* should be described as if they are already happening in the present moment. You can view this piece of writing as a type of a-day-in-the-life-of account. For instance, what would it feel like to be in that room after it was redesigned? What would you do there?

Blastation subscribers can use www.InteractiveLifeCoach.com to create *Big Picture Visions* with both photographic images and text. This way, you'll be able to access them at any time.

Mile Steps

To eat an elephant, you would need to consume him one single bite at a time. The whole shebang would be a bit daunting. Well, in *Blast Off!* language, the bites would be the *Mini Feats*—the daily palatable steps to the *Big Picture Vision* of "eating the elephant."

However, before you could begin to eat the elephant, you'd have to *catch it!* This would be a **Mile Step**. The *Mile Steps* are in between your *Big Picture Vision* and your *Mini Feats*. *Mile Steps* are those large projects, plans and undertakings that work together to reach your *Big Picture Vision*. There may be many or only a few.

Mile Steps are your execution of larger, loftier goals, such as finishing a class, completing an internship, or earning your degree. Once you complete each *Mile Step,* you are closer to reaching your *Big Picture Vision*—your large targeted goal (in this case, starting a new career).

Here's the breakdown:

Big Picture Vision

  divided into *Mile Steps*

    divided into a minimum of three daily *Mini Feats.*

      Then the *Mini Feats* **lead you to** *Miles Steps* **to achieve your** *Big Picture Vision.*

Once you have created your *Big Picture Vision,* ponder on what your *Mile Steps* would be. Look at your *Big Picture Vision* and figure out the main things that have to happen to make this vision a reality. These are your *Mile Steps*!

Then take your *Mile Steps* and break them down into weeks, months or years of *Mini Feats.* You can do this one week at a time, or one day at a time. However you choose to implement the program is completely and utterly fine. Just as long as you do it!

The **Mile Step Spreadsheet** at the back of this workbook can help you break your *Mile Steps* down to the three-a-day *Mini Feats.*

Don't worry if you're not sure how you want to use the various tools and practices right now. The chapters ahead will assist you in working with the Blast Off! Program *to develop your vision for the various areas of your life.*

Get Ready to Blast Off!

The *Blast Off! Program* is comprehensive. Because of its wide-ranging positive impacts, it is important to complete the entire process so that you will reach your goals and ingrain your *Daily Launch Tools* as new healthy habits for your life. Just as exercise has an accumulative impact, so does this program. Though you'll see some initial improvements from taking positive action, the bulk of the program's benefits will come after a month or two of consistent effort and sweat.

I say "sweat" because some of the practices may trigger emotions or resistance. If this happens, it means that you're on the right path. Now before you slam this book shut, let me explain. Facing our true self can be revealing, and often scary. However, once you move through the fear, a huge sense of relief and an empowering new ownership of your personal freedom will be actualized. Yes, the freedom to choose a life full of abundance, soul and adventure is yours for the taking!

With all that said, please make sure that you enjoy the ride. And know that your *Blast Off!* will help you to thrive and prosper. It will give your life passion and meaning.

Finally, we are all on this life path together, learning as we go. So be sure to remember this...

Every new day is an opportunity to start fresh. Don't waste one moment of your life waiting for the right time, or wondering "what if?" There's no better time to launch than now!

"I have learned, that if one advances confidently in the direction of his dreams, and endeavors to live the life he has imagined, he will meet with a success unexpected in common hours."

~Henry David Thoreau,
Author, transcendentalist,
naturalist and philosopher
(1817-1862)

How To Create Your Own
Blast Off! Launching Group

Choose people to work with that are at your level or a level above you in reaching your life goals. Each member of the group can act as a catalyst for inspiration and support. If you are surrounding yourself with people that are not willing to do the work and make the necessary changes in their lives, there is a great possibility that you may become stuck or feel held back.

> "You lift me, and I lift you, and we ascend together."
> *~Anonymous*

Don't be afraid to reach out of your comfort zone and ask people to join your group that are out of your daily life realm. If someone has already achieved a great deal in their lives, it may be time for them to take everything to the next level. This group is the perfect launching pad for this.

I call the groups *Blast Off! Launching Groups* because working through the book while involved in a cohesive group will literally propel each of you to create the dreams and goals you are ready to manifest and achieve.

I recommend anywhere from four to eight people in each group. If there are too many members, each person's share time becomes limited and the meetings will go on too long.

Each *Blast Off! Launching Group* should meet every other week at the same time and place to keep a consistency and flow of action, and to prevent confusion on such details.

Choose the focus of the group. For instance, if you want to focus the group on career and finances, you may not want to work through Chapter Five on relationships, Chapter Six on health and Chapter Eight on adventure and amusement.

If you want to focus only on finding your soulmate, you may not work through Chapter Four on career, or Chapter Seven on financial prosperity. The rest of the chapters can work together to benefit your relationships.

I believe that a truly abundant life is creating fullness in all the areas discussed in *Blast Off!*, so working through each chapter together can only benefit you in your highest calling for success and fulfillment.

Requirements for Group Participants:

1. All members need to take a personal pledge to take responsibility for the choices, actions and scenarios in their lives. For change to happen, you must first take a hard look at yourself and be completely honest about your own contribution to every life situation. This does not mean you need to be critical or hard on yourself. It means you should say, "This is what I have done in the past. It is obviously not working for me, so what am I going to do differently now so that I can feel empowered and reach my goals?" Coming to the group and spouting off blame or victimization only weakens your ability to take control of your life and makes you completely dependent on the past. It also brings everyone else down. Your present and future joy and success depends on this shift in personal ownership thinking. No more excuses!

2. All feedback from group members needs to be honest, yet in a positive and supportive manner. The *Blast Off! Launching Group* needs to be an inspiring and uplifting experience for all members. Insight and suggestions from each member are pertinent for the group's success. However, make sure that your suggestions are expressed in a positive manner, rather than judgmental or critical. You want group members to feel comfortable to express themselves.

3. The *Blast Off! Launching Group* is not a therapy group. Although there will be emotional issues and roadblocks that will arise in your success process, this group is not about continuous venting of your emotional baggage. The intent of your *Blast Off! Launching Group* is a supportive, inspirational and strategic gathering of like-minded individuals that are setting an intention and taking action to reach their dreams and goals. Fear and emotions will undoubtedly come up. However, the commitment of the group is to use the principles of *the Blast Off!* book to move everyone forward past their roadblocks to make positive changes and results.

The Blast Off! Launching Group Process:

1. **Set an intention for the meeting.**

   Begin the group meeting by setting a positive intention for the groups process such as, "We are all here to share abundance, creativity and fulfillment in one another's lives and to inspire and ignite one another's greatness."

2. **Set a time limit for each person to share.**

   If you want to keep the sharing time to an hour and you have six people, keep the sharing time to ten minutes each. Assign one member to be aware of the time. Allow a few minutes between each member for ideas, observations, and insight from other group members. Make sure your time keeper is cognizant of the clock during this process as well.

3. **State your *Big Picture Visions* and Goals.**

   As each person shares with the group, state your *Big Picture Visions* in the areas of life that you are working on. In each session, state your progress in forward movement toward these goals since the last meeting. Then state what you plan to complete by the next meeting. Make a commitment, to yourself and the group that reflects your intention to take action. If you are feeling stuck or need support or advice from the group, state this out loud and allow the other members to offer positive insight or suggestions.

4. **Discuss the reading and exercises assigned the previous week.**

   At the end of each share, take a minute or two to discuss the exercises you have worked on and what you have realized through their completion.

5. **Complete your meeting.**

   a) Assign exercises for next meeting.

   Decide as a group what reading and exercises everyone needs to complete by the next meeting. I suggest two exercises per week. The reading and exercises are pertinent for continued growth and success for the members and group as a whole. Utilize them as a guide to launch you past your barriers and to open up a whole new realm of possibilities.

b) Positive conclusion.

End each *Blast Off! Launching Group* meeting with an inspirational quote from the book. Or have everyone make one positive statement (not a discussion) of something they are grateful for in their lives.

CHAPTER 1

BLAST Off!
to a Life of Passion and Meaning

> "Blaze with the fire that is never extinguished."
>
> *~Luisa Sigea de Velasco, Poet, intellectual, humanitarian (1522-1560)*

A powerful yet energetic flow occurs in your body and mind when you're completely in sync with your emotions, your mental focus, and your actions. Runners experience this as an adrenaline high when their gait pattern is in rhythm with their breath, and they're running at a rapid pace with almost no effort at all. When you're madly in love with what you're doing, something I call your *Secret Spark* will ignite, and you'll experience life with joy in your heart. Even work will no longer feel like work, and you would do it for free if you had to. This is passion!

The practices in Chapter One will assist you in tapping into your passion so that you can begin to soar toward the *Supersonic* realm.

Blast Off! PRACTICE 1: Design Your Own *Personal Life Path*

In the blank space provided in this workbook, write a description of or draw your own *Personal Life Path*. Be as detailed as possible. Your path can be as elaborate or as simple as you choose. No artistic skill is required!

Next, keep your workbook within reach, and whether you feel stuck, get frustrated, or are cruising along in the *Supersonic* space, you can look at your path artwork or description and ask yourself, "Where am I on my *Personal Life Path*?" ✪

Sample drawing of a Personal Life Path

_____

_____

_____

_____

_____

_____

_____

_____

_____

_____

_____

_____

_____

_____

PRACTICE 1: Sketch your own Personal Life Path.

Blast Off! PRACTICE 2: Where Are You Now?

Now I'm going to ask you to evaluate where you are on your *Personal Life Path*. When you think about this, you can include your career, relationships, financial state, health, personal fulfillment and spiritual life. Peruse this list of adjectives and ask yourself which one or two describes where you are on your path.

* Stuck
* Trapped
* Drained
* Frustrated
* Indecisive
* Unmotivated
* Bored
* Exploring new options

* Confused about what direction to take
* At a plateau, enjoyable but ready for more
* So far so good, but time for the next level
* Successful
* Fulfilling
* Inspiring and exciting
* *Supersonic Wow!*

In one of your *Sun-Up Script* writing practices (this is a free-association writing exercise which was described earlier with the other *Daily Launch Tools*), jot down the theme word or words from above that best match your status on your *Personal Life Path*. Write this at the top of a page in your journal, the workbook, or in the *Blastation* software. Then write a page or two about how this word or words describes your situation. At the end, write about how you would like to be different, and what you plan to do to make that change. If you don't know what to do to make the changes, not to worry. This book will be your guide through the changes that are needed. For now, you could just write about your excitement related to working with the *Blast Off! Program*. Next, write your *Rocket Words* (as described below) for the week, summarizing a positive feeling, truth or action related to changing.

> **For example:** *If you chose the word "stuck," write a page or two about how, what and why this stuckness is present and what it represents in your life. Then at the end, write about the opposite of stuck, such as free, open, growing, and what that would feel like if it were really true. Then your* **Rocket Words** *from the Theme Word, stuck, could be:* **"I feel free, light and in motion in every choice and action in my life."** ✪

Blast Off! PRACTICE 3: Proclamation of the Day

Keep your *Rocket Words* (from Practice 2) in your wallet, near your computer, or on your bathroom mirror for a constant reminder of the expansive life you're beginning to create. Read this to yourself and out loud throughout the week. ✪

> "Fill your mind with light, happiness, hope, feelings of security and strength, and soon your life will reflect these qualities."
>
> ~*Remez Sasson,*
> *Author of* Peace of Mind in Daily Life

Blast Off! PRACTICE 4: Let Go, Grow and Change

Resentment, anger and frustration keep us from moving forward in life. These feelings make sure that we stay connected to the past and to our negative situations and relationships. They can wreak havoc with your health and demeanor and at the same time block any potential for joy. If you want to move toward your potential for success, empowerment and love, you will need to begin to release this pain. Just dwelling on the past will keep you stuck there, and I know you want to make a positive shift in your life. It's not a simple task to let go, especially when this person or situation creates a trigger or charge in your energy field.

Just remember that the anger or grief you generate and carry regarding someone else will only mirror the same frequency of energy back to you. So rather than hurting them, you are really hurting yourself. Come on already! Haven't you been through enough?

Take a moment to ask yourself the questions below. In the workbook, write down the immediate thoughts that come to mind without censoring them. Be honest with yourself.

★ What resentments, anger and grief am I carrying around each day?

★ Who am I angry or resentful toward?

★ How can I take responsibility for this situation?

★ What have I learned from this situation that has been positive toward my growth?

★ Can I give myself permission to let go of these negative feelings?

★ How do I feel now that this energy-draining emotion is released?

_____

_____

_____

_____

_____

_____

If you have gotten this far, you are definitely ready for change. You are working diligently to release the past and any negative blocks or energy that have held you back. You are letting go of any burdensome weight that could be slowing your progress. Once it is released, you'll feel like a hundred pounds of grief and stress have melted away. It's true; you'll actually feel physically lighter, freer and more present in the moment. And just think about how much more energy you'll have once you aren't working so hard to hold on to this negative load.

You may be thinking, how can I just let it go? In actuality, it is much easier to let something go, than to hold on to it. Try lifting up something heavy. Feel the effort that it takes to keep the object suspended. How much energy does it take for you to grip the object? How many other body parts are involved? Your entire arm, your torso and your legs are probably all affected from this holding on—all in the effort to keep your equilibrium. Now, let it go. You can do it! Simply release your grip. (Please do not drop anything breakable and find a forgiving surface for the fall.)

Which movement took the least effort? Letting go is effortless. The illusion that letting go is hard is only the mental mania that we give it. Holding on is painful and often results in the exact thing we were trying to avoid—more pain! Well, here's an important truth: *When we allow the past to be in the past, we are making room for new positive energy and circumstances to appear.*

Now that you have let go of past resentments, your focus can shift to the present and the future. Congratulations… you are in motion again! Moving forward rather than hovering is energizing. The momentum feels productive which, in turn, gives you a sense of accomplishment. This is an uplifting place to be. ✪

> "Blaming only gives away our power.
> Keep your power… the helpless
> victim cannot see a way out."
>
> ~*Louise L. Hay,*
> *Author of* You Can Heal Your Life

Blast Off! PRACTICE 5: Accessing Your *Secret Spark*

The following four steps will help you access your *Secret Spark*.

1. **Inspiration Station:** Create an *Inspiration Station* in your home. An *Inspiration Station* is a special space you will create for yourself that is quiet, uncluttered, relaxing and soothing. It can also be encompassed with inspiring elements that will trigger your imagination, creativity and ultimately your *Secret Spark* of passion and meaning. This space needs to reflect the results you are intending to create.

   Your *Inspiration Station* is a place to go to regularly in order to clear your mind so that inspiration will easily appear. To this end, find a quiet space in your home. Decorate it in a calming yet enlivening way that will assist in shifting you to a meditative or creative state, depending on what that visit is calling for.

2. **The *Secret Spark List*:** While sitting in your new inspiring space, make a *Secret Spark List* in the workbook of all the things that you loved to do for fun in childhood. Also, list the things that you would love to try, but never have because of fear or lack of opportunity. These activities can be fun or career-related. You can even include intriguing activities that you have read about, seen on television, or noticed others doing. Break out of the box and be bold in your list. Envision doing things you would never have thought possible. No limits due to money, time or capability apply!

   For example:

   ★ Run in the rain
   ★ Fly a kite
   ★ Finger paint
   ★ Go back to college
   ★ Take hang-gliding lessons
   ★ Write and record a song
   ★ Write a book
   ★ Start a Web-design business

   ★ Get a patent on my great idea
   ★ Practice meditation
   ★ Go on an African safari
   ★ Run a marathon
   ★ Learn Italian
   ★ Open a restaurant
   ★ Play the clarinet
   ★ Live part-time in another country

Take as much time as you need with this list until it feels complete. Visit a bookstore or do some career, adventure or travel searches online. Bookstores and the Web are both good sources of *Secret Spark* inspiration.

_____

_____

_____

_____

_____

_____

_____

_____

_____

_____

_____

_____

_____

_____

_____

_____

_____

_____

_____

_____

_____

_____

_____

_____

3. **The *Secret Spark* Meditation.** Prepare to sit comfortably in your *Inspiration Station*. To relax your mind, you might turn on some soothing music and light some candles. When you're ready to settle down, sit in a relaxed manner and close your eyes. Take a deep, long inhalation through your nose to fill your lungs with oxygen and expand your abdomen. As you exhale, feel any tension leaving your body from your head to your toes. To further relax your spinning mind, visualize all of your day's stresses or worries floating off in a bottle far, far away.

    Once you're feeling quite relaxed and present in the moment, visualize yourself doing one of the activities on your list. Whether your vision is climbing Mount Everest, flying a plane, taking a walk on the beach, or playing with your dog, see yourself immersed in this activity. Feel the environment surrounding you. Hear the sounds and smell the scents of the landscapes. Feel the movement in your body. See yourself performing the activity as if it is really happening in this very moment. Feel the joy, peace, expansion or excitement that this activity brings.

    Do this exercise once a week until one or two of the activities completely resonates with you.

4. **Immerse yourself further through writing.** After the meditation, write about the activity or goal in detail in this workbook or in your journal. Include what it would feel like to create, participate in and accomplish it. Be very specific in your description, such as, "I feel myself breathing under water as I am scuba diving in Hawaii. I am surrounded by hundreds of colorful fish, beautiful coral, and playful dolphins." Write in the present tense as if the activity is happening right now. Read it out loud. Also, feel it in your body as if it is already happening. Believe it to be true! Keep your workbook or journal by your bed and read about the activity or goal first thing when you wake up in the morning and right before closing your eyes to sleep. This will jump-start your unconscious mind into creating ideas and opportunities to make this fun activity or the goal a reality in your life.

By focusing your mindset on invigorating activities, you're activating your mind, body and soul in an inspirational vibration, your *Supersonic gear*. You are also opening the channels for your *Secret Spark* to be revealed. Your life will begin to transform in a way you never thought possible. Walking and exploring with passion in your heart is like being reborn every single day. ✪

> "Wherever you go, go with all your heart."
>
> ~*Confucius,*
> *Chinese philosopher*
> *(551 BC - 479 BC)*

BLAST Off! Daily Launch Tools

1. Each morning, write your *Sun-Up Script* and *Rocket Words*.

2. Read your *Rocket Words* to yourself and out loud as often as possible during your day.

3. Create and perform a minimum of *Mini Feats* each day. (These are the smaller steps for moving toward your larger *Mile Step* goals and your *Big Picture Vision*.) For example, today's *Mini Feats* might be:

- *Download a song I love to be my theme song for my life changes.*
- *Call to sign up for series of dance or acting classes.*
- *Buy an autobiography on Amazon.com of a person who will inspire me while I make my career changes.*

4. Choose one to two *Blast Off! Practices* from this chapter to do each day over the next week.

5. Fill out your *Weekly Flight Assessment Log* to review your week's progress toward realizing your *Supersonic Life*. (You'll find the log form in the back of this book.)

"Love what you do. Do what you love."

~Wayne Dyer,
Self-help author and lecturer

CHAPTER 2

BLAST Off!
to Soulful Living

> "We are not human beings having a spiritual experience; we are spiritual beings having a human experience."
>
> ~Pierre Teilhard de Chardin, French philosopher (1881-1955)

Have you ever arrived somewhere and had no memory of the drive? If someone was to ask you what you had for dinner on Sunday night, would you remember? Do the days go by so fast that you can hardly recall all the things you do and say? This is called "living in the fringe," which means your reality is one big blur, just moving, doing, sleeping, waking up and moving, doing, sleeping all over again. This is the proverbial hamster wheel that eventually results in boredom, burnout, apathy or depression.

If you have a crazy, hectic lifestyle, you are not alone. I've been there myself, and see this issue impacting many of my clients' lives. For this reason, the practices in Chapter Two were designed to help readers slow down the pace and learn to tap into their inner wisdom to create a more soul-enriching life experience.

Blast Off! PRACTICE 1: Plugging In

Visualize your body attached to a cord that is plugged into a generator. Just pretend that you are receiving your morning dose of 100 kW of positive energy, which is supposed to last you all day. You start the day with a full tank of energy. Let's see where you are at the end of the day after depleting your energy bank with negative energy-drainers.

Take a moment to consider how much negative energy you expend.

Here's an example of an overburdened tank.

Full Tank: 100 kW

Minus Negative Energy-Drainers

Dread concerning the meeting with your boss: 10 kW

Fear about not being able to do a good job: 15 kW

Self-reproach about not cleaning the house: 5 kW

Worry about how you're going to pay for the holiday gifts
  (three months away!): 10 kW

Saying "Yes" when you meant "No" and harboring resentment all day: 25 kW

Obsessing over your date and wondering if you'll ever get together again: 10 kW

Guilt about having that extra serving of mashed potatoes: 10 kW

Total Kilowatts of Energy Left: 15 kW

You've already given away 85 kilowatts and that leaves you with only 15 left to make it through the day. No wonder you're so stressed and tired by 4:00 in the afternoon! You are emptying your tank through negative emotions and beliefs which are creating your reality. Just think what would happen if you replaced this negative focus with positive thoughts and actions.

Now try it yourself on your next full day. Start with the 100 kilowatts again in the morning. But this time, whenever you feel a negative thought coming on, switch it immediately to a positive one, even if it is fake or forced. Eventually, positive thoughts will come more naturally and you'll end the day with lots of reserve in your tank. See how you feel.

Then at night, in the space below, write about your experience of trying Practice 1, and look at how it affected your energy level throughout the day. ✪

_____

_____

_____

_____

_____

_____

_____

_____

_____

_____

_____

_____

_____

_____

_____

_____

_____

_____

_____

_____

_____

_____

"Energy and persistence alter all things."

~Ben Franklin,
Author, printer, statesman, inventor
_(1706-1790)_

Blast Off! PRACTICE 2: Heart Space

Here's a mini-meditation that you can do almost anywhere. It's an easy method to get you into your heart space.

1. Put your hand on your chest, over your heart. Hold it there for a few minutes while breathing in through your nose and out from your mouth.

2. Now visualize yourself in the process of doing a task or a bit of work (folding laundry, sitting in your department meeting). Try to generate a feeling of love or gratitude for this effort. If you're having trouble conjuring up the love, feel the warmth for someone you care about very deeply. (Perhaps not your mother-in-law.) Hold on to that loving feeling for a few minutes until it pervades your body.

3. You might even feel a tingling in your body and lightness in your head. This is your energy shifting from a negative mind space to an open-heart space. In a matter of minutes, your stress level (and blood pressure) will have dropped, your heart will be full, and your burdened feelings of carrying the world on your shoulders will have turned into feelings of weightlessness and gratitude.

4. Continue to hold on to that loving and grateful feeling while shifting your focus back to the task or work. Literally see it from your heart. Think of how much you appreciate having this opportunity, and how capable you are of doing your job well.

5. Now participate in the task or work. If you feel yourself losing this peaceful state, stop, cover your heart again, and access those adoring feelings once more. (I realize that you cannot cover your heart in a business meeting. Instead, take a moment to go inward and access being in the heart space. You might even catch yourself enjoying it.)

6. Take a moment during this exercise to breathe in a sense of pride and fulfillment. You're on course while fueling your positive energy meter.

Be patient. It takes practice. The more you operate from a heart space, the easier it becomes to go with the flow and get into the zone. The next time a crazed moment or heavy job calls your name, you'll be able to respond with strength and ease. ✪

Blast Off! PRACTICE 3: True Choice Meditation

What plans have you set for this day, week or month that you might *not* want to do? To help yourself create a list, ask, "Do I feel good about this commitment?" List the possibly unwanted activities now.

_____

_____

_____

_____

_____

_____

_____

_____

_____

_____

Next, in the blank space provided below, write answers to the following questions regarding your commitments for this week or the coming month.

★ What is the purpose of this activity?

★ Who will benefit from this task?

★ Am I doing it out of true choice or habit?

★ Is the action I'm taking working toward my *Big Picture Vision*?

_____

_____

_____

_____

_____

_____

_____

_____

_____

_____

_____

_____

_____

_____

_____

Now sit or lie down in a quiet place and close your eyes. Take deep breaths until your body relaxes and your mind is clear. Visualize yourself first doing this activity, then imagine cutting this activity out of your life.

Consider the following questions for both of the above scenarios:

★ How does it feel in my body?

★ Do any emotions arise?

★ Do I feel fear, nausea, perspiration or shakiness when I think of deleting this activity from my life?

★ Does the activity work with or against my inner knowingness, personal beliefs, or big-picture goals?

Your body is communicating something to you, and if you really take the time to listen, your intuition or inner wisdom will give you the answers. _Just listen._ You will often hear or feel, _"I don't want this anymore,"_ or _"This feels right."_ The trick is that you not only have to listen to your inner wisdom, but you should also follow its lead. ✪

> "You must learn to be still in the midst of activity,
> and to be vibrantly alive in repose."
>
> ~Indira Gandhi,
> _Prime Minister of India_
> _(1917-1984)_

Blast Off! PRACTICE 4: Tasks to Trash

Now that you're aware of the activities you don't feel in alignment with, let's clarify which ones you definitely plan to keep and which ones need to be dragged to the trash. Then you can work on deleting them from your daily life so you can free up your ever-precious time.

1. **List the activities that you're presently involved in that fit within your** *Big Picture Vision.* These activities should come from a place of true choice and fit into a positive frequency of energy that is propelling you to your goals. They add fuel to energize, support and uplift your new life launch. This is a revealing way to see how many activities throughout your days and weeks are really supporting your flight plan, rather than draining energy away from it.

I'm not saying that you should never watch television or clean your house. And I understand that you cannot drop every unwanted responsibility. But do you really need to be on another committee? Is it serving your soul to have the best yard in the neighborhood? Does it give you true pleasure, or are you doing that to impress someone else? If it's for someone else's approval, delete, delete, delete.

Examples of what might on your "keep list:"

- Training for a marathon
- Taking an accounting class because you're starting your own business
- Meditating
- Standing on the sidelines at your child's soccer game

_____

_____

_____

_____

_____

_____

_____

2. **Now list the activities that you're presently involved in that don't fit within your *Big Picture Vision*.** Which activities aren't coming from a place of true choice? If you're feeling drained and irritable around certain to-dos and your inner self is screaming, "I hate this!" throughout the entire process, it's time to let it go.

Some examples of items that might go on your "let go" list:

■ Babysitting for your neighbor

■ Cleaning your teenager's room

■ Handling work at the office that does not fall within the scope of your position

■ Volunteering for another committee ✪

_____

_____

_____

_____

_____

_____

_____

_____

_____

_____

_____

_____

_____

"Methinks I see the wanton hours flee,
and as they pass, turn round and laugh at me."

~George Villiers,
1st Duke of Buckingham
(1592-1628)

Blast Off! PRACTICE 5: "No Go" Exercise

Let's get to it once and for all. It's time for you muster up that "No Factor" and stand up for yourself.

First, practice the following mirror exercise at least four times a week and you'll be speaking your truth in no time!

1. Stand in front of the mirror and say "NO!" *Say it like you mean it.* You may feel silly and awkward at first. *Get over it.* Feel your voice and demeanor strengthening with each "NO." Try pointing your finger at the mirror to give it more strength and power. (This doesn't mean you need to point at everyone that you say "No" to, but it gives some extra punch to the practice.) Do this once a day when you have some privacy until it feels comfortable to you. You can even do this in the shower (without the mirror, of course).

Also, take these additional steps:

2. The next time someone asks you to do something, respond by saying, "Let me get back to you on that." This gets you off the hook for the moment and prevents you from answering impulsively, and possibly regretting it later. Take some time to get in touch with how you really feel about the request. Close your eyes and imagine yourself doing this task and see how it feels in your body and your heart. If you're getting an ill feeling, that is usually a sign that a good "No" is in order.

3. Now it's time to go for it! Keep that memory of the ill feeling in mind (so you won't cave) as you tell the person that you have decided to pass on their request. If it's something you might want to do at a later time, tell them to keep you in mind at the next go-around. If not, just say, "I really cannot help you out at this time." Your stomach may be churning. *That is normal.* This is a new threshold that you're crossing. Guilt may be popping its ugly head up and saying, "You are so selfish. You're letting everyone down." Tell it to buzz off because there's no room for that wasted emotion anymore.

4. Revel in the achievement and freedom you own after releasing yourself from this unwanted activity. Just think how you'll feel when you begin clearing your days of many unwanted yeses. All of that precious energy that has

gone to activities you didn't really want to be involved in can now flow back to your inner being. And that's not even taking into account the energy that was being drained by the buildup of negative inner feelings.

Congratulations! You've just turned your negative output into positive input. Your health, self-respect and quality time have improved immensely. And much to your surprise, watch how others start to treat you and your time with more respect. ✪

> "The heart is the first feature
> of working minds."
>
> ~Frank Lloyd Wright,
> Architect, writer and educator
> (1867-1959)

Blast Off! PRACTICE 6: No More, No More, No More, No More

After completing Practice 5, make note of all the activities and tasks that you're ready to say "No!" to and start feeling lighter immediately.

Your list will look something like this (but with the blanks filled in):

I am choosing not to _____ anymore.

I am choosing not to _____ anymore.

No, I am choosing not to_____ anymore.

_____

_____

_____

_____

Go ahead. Erase all those unwanted activities and tasks from your to-do list and replace them (guilt free) with true choice activities. Your heart, mind and soul will thank you. Remember, this is not being selfish. When you're happy, those around you will be even happier. It's that simple. ☻

> "Never mistake motion for action."
>
> ~Ernest Hemingway,
> *Pulitzer-Prize-winning novelist,*
> *short story writer, journalist (1899-1961)*

Blast Off! PRACTICE 7: Accessing Your Soul's Choice

I remember doing this exact exercise at that crucial time of change in my life. I also continue to practice it frequently in my life today. Just as we did the **True Choice Meditation** earlier in this chapter, we can utilize this same method in connecting with our Higher Self.

1. Get into your *Inspiration Station* or another quiet space, and close your eyes. Inhale and take a deep breath through your nose. Expand your lungs and feel your abdomen protrude with oxygen-rich air. Then, as you exhale, visualize any confusion, stress or fear leaving your body. Continue this breathing release method until you feel totally relaxed, calm and clear.

2. Now ask a question out loud that is currently on your mind.

    For example:

    ▨ Is this the right career for me?

    ▨ Is this relationship serving my soul and higher purpose?

    ▨ What do I really want to be doing with my life?

    ▨ Am I happy in this situation? If not, how am I feeling? What do I need to do about it?

    ▨ Should I take this trip?

    ▨ Should I take this new job offer?

3. Listen to your inner voice and your long-awaited answers will come. It's a knowing that will permeate in your entire body on a cellular level. If you experience pain somewhere in your body, ask your soul what this means. What are you doing to create this pain in your life and what can you change or do differently to release the pain?

Do you hear the words coming through? What is the message? If you listen closely, it will be ringing in loud and clear.

Make some notes about the messages coming from your inner wisdom here.

_____

_____

_____

_____

_____

_____

_____

_____

_____

_____

_____

_____

_____

_____

The next time you receive the wisdom of your soul, listen and follow it all the way through. Don't run, hide or avoid the truth of your personal path. It may be scary, even terrifying, however walking through the fear will bring you miracles beyond belief. Your soul knows the truest path for you. Follow its lead! ✪

> "There is always a true inner voice—
> Trust it."
>
> ~Gloria Steinem,
> *Journalist, political activist and author of*
> Revolution from Within

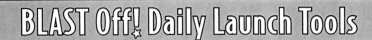

BLAST Off! Daily Launch Tools

1. Each morning, write your *Sun-Up Script* and *Rocket Words*.

2. Read your *Rocket Words* to yourself and out loud as often as possible during your day.

3. Create and perform a minimum of *Mini Feats* each day. (These are the smaller steps for moving toward your larger *Mile Step* goals and your *Big Picture Vision*.) For example, today's *Mini Feats* might be:

- *Before I go to bed read for five minutes from a spiritual or philosophical book that inspires me or helps me to reconnect with life's bigger picture.*

- *Listen to some guided meditation (see Resource section in back of book).*

- *Research, locate and sign up for a local yoga, meditation or t'ai chi class in my area to help bring some soul and sustenance to my days.*

4. Choose one to two *Blast Off! Practices* from this chapter to do each day over the next week.

5. Fill out your *Weekly Flight Assessment Log* to review your week's progress toward realizing your *Supersonic Life*.

"All human beings should try to learn before they die
what they are running from, and to, and why."

~James Thurber,
Humorist and The New Yorker *magazine cartoonist*
(1894-1961)

CHAPTER 3

BLAST Off!
to Limitless
Living

> "You can walk in grace or you can walk in fear, but you can't have it both ways."
>
> ~Carlos Santana,
> Grammy-award-winning
> musician, philanthropist

Your personal universe has no bounds. If you're feeling stuck or trapped in one or more realms of your life, it may be because you have enclosed yourself under an imaginary lid, then fooled yourself into believing that someone or something has forced you to put up with an unfulfilling or even miserable existence. The good news is that if you closed the lid, you also have the ability to unlock and release it. This move will open you up to a limitless universe of opportunities and experiences, as well as the absolute ability to make your wildest dreams come true.

Through the practices in this chapter, you'll learn how to identify where and how you are limiting your potential and what you can do to release your personal lid. Then you'll have the power to completely transform every aspect of your limited world into a wide-open, abundant playground.

Blast Off! PRACTICE 1: Name That Delusion

Let's take a close look at the negative core beliefs you have adopted. Then you can begin to undo the blockage and create magic as you learn to shift the delusions to a completely new and limitless mindset.

In the space below, make a list of the strongest fears or negative beliefs that you live with. (*Blastation* subscribers can do this work on the website at www.InteractiveLifeCoach.com.)

*Creating awareness of your limiting beliefs
is the first step in your upcoming release.* ✪

_____

_____

_____

_____

_____

_____

_____

_____

_____

_____

_____

_____

_____

_____

_____

_____

_____

_____

_____

Blast Off! PRACTICE 2: Choices from Fear

Now that you've listed your core delusions, think about how they have affected the major choices in your life regarding your relationships, careers, financial state, hobbies and values. What are you living now as a result of these negative beliefs?

In a moment, I want you to list your present status in each life sector. But first, look at these examples:

Career: *I am so worried about financial security that I am not really pursuing my dream career. I am not mentally stimulated in my job. In fact, I am so bored at work.*

Relationship: *I have always settled for partners who I knew would not abandon me, even though I wasn't really attracted to them. Then I lose interest and leave.*

Now it's your turn. In the workbook, write two to three sentences about where you are now in the following areas of your life based on any fearful choices or limiting beliefs:

1. Career_____

_____

_____

_____

_____

_____

2. Relationship_____

_____

_____

_____

_____

_____

3. Health _____

_____

_____

_____

_____

4. Financial _____

_____

_____

_____

_____

5. Personal fulfillment _____

_____

_____

_____

_____

6. Spiritual _____

_____

_____

_____

Were you surprised at how many life choices you have made as a result of fear? Mind-boggling, isn't it? ✪

"I have only one life, and it is short enough.
Why waste it on things I don't want most?"

~Louis D. Brandeis,
Supreme court justice
(1856-1941)

Blast Off! PRACTICE 3: Flip-Switching

Now that you've recognized your damaging beliefs and how they have shaped some of the circumstances you're experiencing in your present life, let's "flip the switch"—an exercise in deleting the negative, sabotaging beliefs and thoughts and replacing them with limitless abundant thinking. Then you can begin to "remove the lid" on your life and allow the goodness to appear.

For example:

Core Delusion: *"The world has become so scary."*

Winning Belief: *"The world is safe and full of beautiful and exciting possibilities."*

Core Delusion: *"I must struggle to make money. I'm so tired of living paycheck to paycheck."*

Winning Belief: *"Money is always available to me and my bank account is growing every day."*

Core Delusion: *"I rarely try new things because I'm afraid to fail."*

Winning Belief: *"I enjoy challenging myself because I know that I can achieve whatever I set my mind on doing."*

Core Delusion: *"My friends seem to have the best luck. Meanwhile, I never seem to get what I wish for."*

Winning Belief: *"Opportunities are falling into my lap on a daily basis."*

Core Delusion: *"True love only exists in fairy tales."*

Winning Belief: *"True love is mine for the taking because I deserve it."*

Core Delusion: *"I am timid in gatherings and new situations."*

Winning Belief: *"I am dynamic."*

Core Delusion: *"I feel stuck. My life is boring and unfulfilling."*

Winning Belief: *"My life is fun and full of new adventures."*

Now, from the list of core delusions that you listed in this chapter's *Blast Off! Practice 1*, flip-switch each statement to a positive polar-opposite winning belief. Jot down these winning beliefs in the blank space provided below. (**Hint:** Core delusions are heavy, dense and cumbersome. Winning beliefs are light, expansive and uplifting!) ✪

_____

_____

_____

_____

_____

_____

_____

_____

_____

_____

_____

_____

_____

_____

_____

_____

_____

_____

_____

_____

_____

_____

_____

_____

_____

Blast Off! PRACTICE 4: Visualizing Your Short-Term Goals

The following practice generalizes an envisioning process for realizing any short-term goal. I discuss envisioning in greater detail in the *Blast Off!* book.

1. Write down exactly what you want to achieve regarding your short-term goals.

2. Visualize yourself going through all the motions as you make these goals happen in your limitless mind.

3. Take in the full experience of achieving each goal. See it, feel it, smell it as if you are experiencing it happening *right now*. Get in touch with the energy related to the experience. As you envision the goal, you may experience a reaction in your body and your mind that is like a buzzing or a warm feeling. Combine your wonderful energy with positive thoughts. *Wow, Wow, Wow!*

Commit this process to memory and then repeat it as often as possible. The more positive frequency your dreams receive, the more momentum they will have to take flight. ✪

_____

_____

_____

_____

_____

_____

_____

_____

_____

"We must dare to dream great dreams and then we must dare to put them in action."

~Peter McDonald

Blast Off! PRACTICE 5: Illustrate and Write about Your *Big Picture Vision*

It's time to use your artistry and creativity to set your *Big Picture Vision*. You need not be a Picasso or Shakespeare to do this exercise. Drawing, painting, photography, collage and writing open up your right brain, your imaginative and intuitive side. They're also great ways to release any pent-up emotions that could get in the way of envisioning and actualizing your dreams. If you need to take a red or black crayon and scribble all over a piece of paper first, be my guest. Feel better now?

1. **First, illustrate your vision.** Create images that represent your *Big Picture Vision* for any or all areas of your life, including career, relationship, health, wealth, personal fulfillment and spiritual. **Drawing and painting:** Whether it is a stick person (you) hanging out with the lions in Africa or dining with your lover in your Tuscan villa, get as colorful and as wild as you like. There is blank space in the workbook to create one *Big Picture Vision*, which you can view for inspiration whenever you want. You can also create other *Big Picture Vision* artwork for additional areas of your life. Hang them up in visible places that you spend time in each day. **Desktop:** Subscribers can use the *Blastation* software at www.InteractiveLifeCoach.com to upload and combine digital photographic images to create an illustration of their *Big Picture Vision*. Visit the site as often as you'd like, or make a printout and post it in a highly visible spot.

PRACTICE 5: **Sketch your** *Big Picture Vision.*

Create your *Big Picture Vision Story*. (In other words, write about a day in the life of your *Big Picture Vision*.) Write the story in the first person and in the present tense as if it is happening already. You can create your first *Big Picture Vision* in the space provided, and then use copies of the *Big Picture Vision Board* form from the back of this book for revisions and additional *Big Picture Visions*. Also, note that the *Blastation* software has a feature, too, for this use.

How does it feel to be in your story? What do you see? Who else is there?

Example:

I am standing outside the home we have built for foster children. There are kids of all ages playing on the swings or sitting inside at the computers doing homework.

A little girl comes and puts her hand in mine as I walk into the beautiful stone-and-brick building that is adorned with lots of windows and vibrant greenery. My staff is qualified in child psychology and they are very well paid. They love their work and it shows in how they interact with the children.

_____

_____

_____

_____

_____

_____

_____

_____

_____

_____

_____

_____

_____

_____

_____

_____

_____

_____

_____

_____

_____

_____

_____

_____

_____

_____

_____

_____

_____

_____

_____

_____

_____

2. Read your _Big Picture Vision Story_ out loud as often as possible, as if you are proclaiming it to the Universe. "Let there be light!"

3. Use your _Big Picture Vision_ in the next _Blast Off! Practice._

4. Now that you have more clarity about your _Big Picture Vision,_ start envisioning it into being. ✪

"Life is a verb."

~_Charlotte Perkins Gilman,
Novelist, artist, speaker, social reformer
(1860-1935)_

Blast Off! | PRACTICE 6: Envisioning Your *Big Picture Vision*

When you hook the cables to a car battery to jump-start an engine, you must connect the positive cable clamp to the positive battery charge and the negative cable clamp to the negative battery charge. This like energy ignites power in the dead battery, bringing it to life. This is similar to having high-quality thoughts and a positive vibrational frequency. To jump-start your dream, you must also send it like energy.

1. **First you must relax your body and mind.** The envisioning is going to be much more effective coming from a calm and peaceful energy, rather than a stressed-out, chaotic energy.

2. **Close your eyes and inhale deeply.** As you inhale, envision a glowing white light entering the spot between your eyes (your third eye). As you exhale, feel that rejuvenating energy move from the spot on your forehead and melt down through the inside of your system very slowly. See and feel the white glowing energy filling up every part of your body until your stress is replaced with clear, rejuvenating vigor.

3. **Begin to see yourself actualizing the dream** as if it has already happened. This can be done successfully in two ways. Envision yourself in the process of living your limitless dream, and also envision yourself as the observer of this dream (you observing yourself observing yourself). Both methods work. Seeing yourself inside and outside of your *Big Picture Vision* only creates more positive electricity around it.

4. **Dream big. Envision bigger.** When you visualize your *Big Picture Vision*, think outside the box. Bust through your limiting thoughts and think bigger than you ever imagined possible.

Example: A woman named Karla came to see me for coaching when she didn't know what career path to take after a horse-riding ranch (where she trained young riders) was closed unexpectedly. Karla had become distraught because she loved that job and now she didn't know what to do. She planned to go back to school to become a physical therapist, but just couldn't seem to get too excited about it.

We did some brainstorming and she said her big dream would be to own and operate a rehabilitation ranch for horses. When Karla first thought about it, her eyes instantly lit up with joy and a sense of relief. But once her newly accessed limitless thinking kicked in, I noticed that she became very overwhelmed and fearful at the thought of running a business like this. "I don't think I could ever do that," was her spontaneous limited-thinking remark. Karla said she could just work for another rehab ranch instead.

I knew that Karla was completely capable of actualizing her passion. Choosing to follow her fear, which many people do, would have caused her to settle for something less than what she really wanted. If she sold herself short, Karla's wonderful dream would vanish into Fantasy Land.

We broke down the general **Mile Steps** that would be needed in order to open a small rehab facility. From there, we simplified the steps even more into palatable **Mini Feats**. (See the **Mile Steps Spreadsheet** in the back of this book which was designed to walk you through this process.) Through this technique, Karla didn't feel that the dream was too daunting to achieve. For the first time in a very long while, she felt excited and impassioned about her future. She now had a direction with manageable steps to follow. The biggest hurdle she overcame that day was breaking through her limiting thinking and then seeing and believing that it was really possible to realize her dream. Now she could envision and actualize the horse rehab center into her life.

5. Not only do you need to see yourself in the process of this dream... you need to **feel it in every cell of your body**. Feel your senses open and your breathing deepen, as you allow your body and mind to feel this *Big Picture Vision* become a reality.

6. **Stay with that picture** and those thoughts as long as possible. The more time you emit those positive *Wow Frequencies* toward the life design that you have in mind, the more focused the energy will be in manifesting your dreams.

7. **Then let it go.** Remember that the best things in life come as a surprise. Think about it. When you consider the most wonderful happenings in your life, there's a good chance that they weren't planned, but were unexpectedly dropped into your lap by Ms. Universe herself. So envision it, feel it, and then

set your dream free. Allow the way that your dream comes to you to be a surprise. Remember, holding on to expectations too tightly will only cause them to slip through your fingers.

8. **Create a good mantra.** A mantra is a sacred word or phrase used as a repeated chant that helps to facilitate spiritual or personal growth. Create one for yourself now, and write it in the space below. In Karla's case, it could be on the theme of empowerment.

Here's an example of a **Phrase Mantra:** *My limits are dissolving at this very moment and my limitless life is already at work unfolding in a miraculous way.* Another could be: *All my dreams are coming true.*

_____

_____

_____

_____

_____

_____

_____

_____

_____

_____

After working with this practice, you'll have uplifting thoughts and feelings about your *Big Picture Vision* that you will emit into the Universe every day. This will be a big step toward creating your limitless life! ✪

> "Somewhere, something incredible
> is waiting to be known."
>
> ~Carl Sagan,
> *Astronomer, author, host of the TV series* Cosmos
> *(1934-1996)*

BLAST Off! Daily Launch Tools

1. Each morning, write your *Sun-Up Script* and *Rocket Words*.

2. Read your *Rocket Words* to yourself and out loud as often as possible during your day.

3. Create and perform a minimum of *Mini Feats* each day. (These are the smaller steps for moving toward your larger *Mile Step* goals and your *Big Picture Vision*.) For example, today's *Mini Feats* might be:

   - *Take one small risk every day this week, including, ask my boss for a raise, call a certain someone (who I have avoided) about getting together, and speak up and ask for something that I really want.*

   - *Choose a certain action that I have avoided out of fear. (Make this your first* Mini Feat *of the week. No more excuses!)*

   - *Research on the Internet about the new industry I'm interested in.*

4. Choose one to two *Blast Off! Practices* from this chapter to do each day over the next week.

5. Fill out your *Weekly Flight Assessment Log* to review your week's progress toward realizing your *Supersonic Life*.

"Change your thoughts
and you change your world."

~*Norman Vincent Peale,*
Minister, motivational speaker, and author of The Power of Positive Thinking
(1898-1993)

CHAPTER 4

BLAST Off!
to the Career of Your Dreams

Have you known for some time what you are meant to do for a career, but you just aren't sure how to transfer it to real life? Are you still searching for that path you can call your very own? Everyone was blessed with certain gifts, talents and personality traits that can be transferred into a fulfilling, satisfying and financially prosperous line of work. Some people (as I discussed in the first chapter of *Blast Off!*) know from the get-go what they want to be when they grow up. Others, like me, find their purpose through an evolution of life's experiences and challenges. Either way, you can develop a career that is perfectly right for you.

The practices in Chapter Four will help you explore your interests, values and career options, then guide you to setting yourself up for higher levels of wealth.

> "Make no little plans; they have no magic to stir men's blood.... Make big plans; aim high in hope and work."
>
> ~Daniel Burnham, Architect, urban planner and the designer of the famous Flatiron Building in New York City (1846-1912)

Blast Off! PRACTICE 1: Ignite Your Right Brain

Choose from one of the following tools to stimulate your creative right-brain hemisphere: (1) meditation, (2) art, (3) listening to Baroque music, (4) physical exercise, (5) bodywork, (6) homeopathy, color therapy or aromatherapy (see the main book *Blast Off!* for background on each). Try a new method each week and see which ones work best for you. Keep them in your repertoire for use at times when you're feeling stuck or in need of some creative inspiration and motivation. ✪

"Whatever the mind can conceive and believe,
it can achieve."

~Napoleon Hill,
American author, and one of the earliest
writers of personal success literature
(1883-1970)

Blast Off! PRACTICE 2: What Path Should I Take?

You know you want to make a change. You want to find a new direction that is inspiring and fulfilling. The following **Dream Career Questionnaire** can spark some ideas to help you get started. Write your answers in the workbook, or within the *Blastation* software at the website www.InteractiveLifeCoach.com.

1. **As a child, what did you dream of being when you grew up?** It's helpful to get in touch with your earlier fascinations. In early childhood, it was easier to live from our imagination without all of the interference from our adopted limiting beliefs.

   _____

   _____

   _____

   _____

   _____

   _____

2. **What are some of your favorite hobbies or activities—in the present and in the past—and why?** Wouldn't it be great if you could turn your favorite pastime into your dream career? We choose hobbies and activities that most likely resonate with our unique personality, as well as our physical, mental and emotional nature. They are an extension of our inner voice and a *Blast Off!* to your dream career.

   _____

   _____

   _____

   _____

   _____

3. **What do you do, or have you done, in your life that makes you the happiest? What is it about this that you enjoy so much? What does it mean to you?** When you are in a state of joy or bliss, you are in complete alignment with your purpose. And when you're in complete alignment with your passions, intention and actions, success is sure to follow.

_____

_____

_____

_____

_____

_____

4. **What things have you always wanted to do, but were afraid to try?** These could be activities or ideas related to your personal life or career that you have seen on television, in books, or heard of others experiencing. List anything that comes to mind that seems interesting, stimulating, exciting, meaningful or fun.

As I outlined in Chapter Three, many people self-impose limiting choices and circumstances on themselves and their lives. Once those obstacles are removed, the possibilities are boundless. People often fear change, even if their current circumstances are not up to par with their capabilities. The hardest part of change is the first step. Once you get through that, creating your new and successful career becomes so much easier. The fear will be released the more you practice taking action.

_____

_____

_____

_____

_____

_____

_____

5. **What is a cause that you could get behind?** Is there a cause or charity that you're passionate about? There may be some career ideas that will support and reflect the charities or causes that have meaning to you.

One of my clients, Leslie, felt stuck for years in a job that offered no challenge or mental stimulation whatsoever. She was very over-qualified for the position, but stayed for the security. As the years went by, Leslie became more and more apathetic toward her work. In the meantime, she was taking classes in homeopathy for animals, and volunteering at the local animal shelter. It was obvious that humane treatment and care for animals was a cause that she felt very strongly about. It never felt like work because she absolutely loved to connect with the animals. Over time, Leslie began practicing natural medicine for animals on a part-time basis until she developed enough business to take the leap in creating her full-time dream career. Now, instead of going to her boring job, she wakes up each day to a dream career that she is most passionate about. She successfully moved her professional status from the *Floating Stage* to *Supersonic*.

_____

_____

_____

_____

6. **What values do you hold most important in your life?** If you can incorporate some of the most important values of your character and your life into your work, you will be truly living a life of value and purpose. For example, I have always felt a calling to help people in need. At some point, I finally reconnected with my deeper values and life purpose to support and inspire others on their path. Life coaching was a natural evolution because it matched my inner values and purpose.

_____

_____

_____

_____

7. **What are your strengths and talents?** By tapping into the special abilities that you were born with, you can consider translating them into your dream career. My client, Kenneth, loves parasailing, so he is creating a charity that will help trauma victims heal through this sport. He has found a way to combine his passion and talent to give back to a cause he feels strongly about.

_____

_____

_____

_____

_____

_____

_____

_____

_____

_____

8. **What movies and books have inspired you over the years, and why?** We are often drawn to books and movies that reflect our personalities and interests. For example, history books may reflect your interest in travel or research. Action/adventure books and movies may mirror your desire for a career in an outdoor setting, rather than being office-bound.

_____

_____

_____

_____

_____

_____

_____

_____

9. **What does success mean to you?** Success can have many different connotations and can represent different things to different people. What does the picture of success look like to you?

_____

_____

_____

_____

_____

_____

_____

10. **If you had plenty of money at your disposal to invest in your own dream career, what kind of business would you start?** Often the fear of not having enough capital, or an inheritance, or just-accepting-poverty thinking can dissuade people from reaching for their dreams. As I mention in _Blast Off!_ repeatedly, just by putting your dreams on paper, sending your intention out into the Universe, and following up with action, the necessary avenues to remove these supposed limitations will appear. This is intention in action. There are also many resources for small-business funding. Don't let the financial aspect stop you, because there will always be a solution if you actively look for it. The secret is to profess your dream, and then start taking action toward it today. You may begin to receive unexpected checks in the mail. Stranger things have happened! The Universe has incredible ways of providing for us once we put out the intention, then _believe_ that it will appear.

_____

_____

_____

_____

_____

_____

Upon completion of *Blast Off! Practice 2*, look at each of your answers to the questionnaire. Do you see a common theme throughout? This is a very good clue for your winning dream career. For instance, if all your answers have to do with creative activities, you may fit with a career in the arts, such as landscape design, interior design, fine art or graphic design. If you see travel dominating your answers, a career as a travel agent, excursion director, or editor of a travel magazine may be the fuel for your *Secret Spark*.

These answers will reflect your inner purpose. A dream career that expresses your values, hopes, loves and dreams is a winning recipe for victory. ✪

"Success is your dreams
with work clothes on."

~Anonymous

Blast Off! | PRACTICE 3: Brainstorming Your Dream Career

Now write down all your common themes from the *Dream Career Questionnaire* on the left side of the space below. From these themes, write down any dream career ideas adjacent to them on the right. (*Blastation* subscribers can do this work at www.InteractiveLifeCoach.com.)

Here are some examples:

Inner Purpose Themes	Dream Career Ideas
Travel	Director of travel adventure company
Design	Interior design, architecture, landscaping ✪

_____

_____

_____

_____

_____

_____

_____

_____

_____

_____

_____

_____

_____

_____

_____

_____

_____

_____

_____

_____

_____

Blast Off! PRACTICE 4: Your *Dream Career Mission Statement*

Now that you have some idea of what type of career you want to create or embark on, it's time to formulate the purpose of that dream career in your *professional mission statement*.

Here's an example of a *professional mission statement*:

Blast Off! Life Coaching *(www.MyBlastOff.com) is a consulting service that coaches individuals and companies on a one-on-one and group basis to inspire a vision, create a direction, and implement plans of action to meet and exceed long-term goals in all aspects of life.* Blast Off! Life Coaching *is committed to supporting its clients' dreams, personal and fiscal goals, human spirit, health and inner peace for a most abundant and prosperous life. As the Director for* Blast Off! Life Coaching, *I promise to be a catalyst for people to understand and reach their true potential.*

Now create your own personal or career mission statement in the space below. ✪

_____

_____

_____

_____

_____

_____

_____

_____

_____

_____

_____

_____

_____

_____

_____

_____

Blast Off! PRACTICE 5: State Your Plates and Platters

Once you have developed your dream career idea, you'll want to take a hard look at the numbers so you can manifest more wealth into your life. The more aware you are, the better off you'll be. Review and check in with these numbers frequently. Adjust them accordingly. Hopefully upwards! (*Blastation* subscribers can do this work on the website www.InteractiveLifeCoach.com.)

Blue Plate Special Number (Survival Number): This is how much money you need to make just to survive and pay the bills and taxes each month.

★ Make a list of all your monthly expenses, including your mortgage or rent, utilities, food, clothing, personal affects, other current bills, taxes and so on.

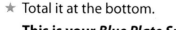

★ Total it at the bottom.
This is your *Blue Plate Special Number.*
$

Silver Platter Number (Exceeding Survival): This is a goal that's higher than what you're reaching now.

★ Take the same financial budget from your *Blue Plate Special Number* and increase the numbers in areas where you wish to be able to spend more. For instance, if you spend $100 per month for personal care, such as massage or gifts, you may want to increase that to $500 or $1,000 in your *Silver Platter*. You can also add categories that you couldn't afford in your *Blue Plate Special Number*, such as travel or entertainment.

_____

_____

_____

_____

_____

_____

_____

_____

_____

_____

_____

_____

_____

_____

_____

_____

_____

_____

_____

★ Total it at the bottom.

This is your *Silver Platter Number*.

$

Gold Platter Number (Your *Blast Off! Number*): This is your ultimate financial goal.

⭐ Take the same financial budget from your *Silver Platter Number* and increase the numbers in areas where you wish to be able to spend more. For instance, you may want to add a category for your fantasy trip around the world. You may want to build your dream home. Figure your approximate total expense and break it into a monthly budget. Remember, this is what you are working towards. You do not have to know how or when this money will arrive yet. Be patient. Believe and take action. It will come.

_____

_____

_____

_____

_____

_____

_____

_____

_____

_____

_____

_____

_____

_____

_____

_____

_____

_____

⭐ Total it at the bottom.

This is your Gold Platter Number.

$

I have written my *Silver* and *Gold Platter Numbers* each quarter over the past several years. By simply listing these each quarter or each year, you're setting an intention that you are expecting to achieve these financial goals. Then take action through your *Mini Feats* to bring these numbers into reality. I am always pleasantly surprised when I add up the income for the year and look back at my intentions. It works. I'm telling you, it really works! ✪

"You must seek wealth for it to seek you."

~*John Demartini,*
Author of The Breakthrough Experience
and The Riches Within

BLAST Off! Daily Launch Tools

1. Each morning, write your *Sun-Up Script* and *Rocket Words*.

2. Read your *Rocket Words* to yourself and out loud as often as possible during your day.

3. Create and perform a minimum of *Mini Feats* each day. (These are the smaller steps for moving toward your larger *Mile Step* goals and your *Big Picture Vision*.) For example, today's *Mini Feats* might be:

   - *Perform some market research. Research industry websites that pique my interest.*

   - *Check out a local business networking group or chamber of commerce event. Ask people who share my interests about their careers. (You will be amazed at the good information you'll receive.)*

   - *Sign up for Toastmasters to improve my self-confidence in speaking. (This will enhance your interviews, and sales, and of course help you to overcome the great phobia of public speaking.)*

   - *Set a firm date that I will be making a change in my job or starting a business on the side. (Make that commitment to yourself. Start walking toward your* Big Picture Vision *now.)*

4. Choose one to two *Blast Off! Practices* from this chapter to do each day over the next week.

5. Fill out your *Weekly Flight Assessment Log* to review your week's progress toward realizing your *Supersonic Life*.

"Only those who risk going too far
can possibly find out how far one can go."

~T. S. Elliott,
Poet, playwright and literary critic, took the Nobel Prize for Literature in 1948
(1888-1965)

BLAST Off!
to the "Love-of-Your-Life" Relationship

> "If you wished
> to be loved, love."
>
> ~Lucius Annaeus Seneca,
> Roman philosopher,
> playwright, statesman
> (4 BC-65 AD)

Can you relate to this scenario? A potential partner comes along who has some of the qualities you desire, but there are some glaring differences that raise those telltale red flags from the beginning. Still, you try to ignore them. Well, if this has been your pattern, you're not alone. I have many clients who come to me complaining about their relationships. When we break down the issues, it's apparent that one or both individuals have settled for one reason or another.

I'm not saying that a relationship cannot grow and thrive if every single aspect of both partners is not a match. However, if you have to convince yourself that you really don't need those elements in your life, you may be settling for second, third, fourth or fifth best. I know from my own personal experiences, and from those of my clients, that we can talk ourselves into situations that we realize are not right from the beginning because we feel, at a core level, that we either do not deserve someone better, or that the person of our dreams just doesn't exist.

Chapter Five's practices will help you realize your worth, become more welcoming, and think through what you really want and need in a relationship. Then you can plan the steps to bring love your way, set your intention on finding your match by a certain date, and begin envisioning your dream love life into reality.

Blast Off! PRACTICE 1: What Inner Language Are You Projecting?

In my own dating situation, I kept thinking, "I'm not acting needy. I'm not clinging to these relationships. What's the deal?" I cried to the heavens, "Why is all this rejection happening?" Outwardly I was cool, calm and collected. It was obvious that I was very independent in my career and completely capable of taking care of my child on my own. Nevertheless, the energy of my unconscious little girl longing for love was screaming out loudly and desperately.

To be able to finally draw in the love and relationship you desire, you must first recognize what energy or behavior you are projecting. What is your inner language expressing without saying anything at all? Get into a quiet space or your *Inspiration Station* and ask yourself straight out, "What is my inner language saying to the world?" Listen to your inner voice and the answers will come. Do not candy-coat them. The more honest you are with yourself, the more powerful and positive the changes will be. Make a written record of the answers that come to you in the space below, and refer to it as you work on shifting and lifting your energy. ✪

_____

_____

_____

_____

_____

_____

_____

_____

_____

_____

_____

Blast Off! PRACTICE 2: My True Self Revealed

People often suppress their true identity and their needs in an effort to attain love and security. The truth is that the love and security you receive in this manner is most likely an illusion, because it is a result of self-fear, not self-love. Until we live our lives congruently, meaning our inner truth must equal outer action, we cannot find peace, love and happiness.

In the space below, make a list of all your glorious inner and outer qualities that you would want to be recognized and loved by a soulmate. ✪

_____

_____

_____

_____

_____

_____

_____

_____

_____

_____

_____

_____

_____

_____

"People often say that 'beauty is in the eye of the beholder,'
and I say that the most liberating thing about beauty
is realizing that you are the beholder.
This empowers us to find beauty in places where
others have not dared to look, including inside ourselves."

~Salma Hayek,
Actress who starred in Frida *and* Fools Rush In

Blast Off! PRACTICE 3: Your Soulmate Shopping List and Soulmate Statement

Think deeply and honestly about what's most important to you in a partner and then make your own **Soulmate Shopping List.** Record the list in the space below in the workbook, or in the *Blastation* software at www.InteractiveLifeCoach.com.

What are all the qualities you want to have in a relationship, even if something might seem trivial to someone else? Only *you* know what you're attracted to and what your needs, desires and values are. It's time you get what you so beautifully deserve. **Do Not Write What You Don't Want.** By doing that, you would be still projecting energy out toward what you don't want. **Only List What You Do Want.** This will set your intention.

For example:

★ Is close to my age.

★ Loves to travel.

★ Is good with children.

★ Is ready for a relationship.

★ Etc., etc.

If you have already been blessed with finding your Soulmate, your relationship can continue to grow and evolve. A tool to help you do this is the *Big Picture Vision* for your relationship, what I call the *Soulmate Statement*. Your *Soulmate Statement* will be a story about the two of you enjoying the current state that you would like to be in. By describing you and your partner in this ideal state, you will begin to make shifts in your relationship without having to do or say anything.

Use the blank space below to write your *Soulmate Statement* or you can create it in the *Blastation* at www.InteractiveLifeCoach.com. Later versions of handwritten *Soulmate Statements* can be created on copies of the *Big Picture Vision Board* form from the back of the workbook.

Read your *Soulmate Statement* every day, see and feel yourself and your partner in this positive state, and watch the changes unfold!

If you're actively looking for your soulmate, your next step is to also write a *Soulmate Statement.* Use the space below in the workbook, or create it in the *Blastation* software. (There is also the *Big Picture Vision Board* form in the back of this book that you can use for later versions.) Address how you would like to be together. Include how you would act toward one another, where the two of you would go, what you would do, etc. As mentioned above, this represents the *Big Picture Vision* of your relationship. ✪

_____

_____

_____

_____

_____

_____

_____

_____

_____

_____

_____

_____

_____

_____

_____

_____

"Grow old along with me! The best is yet to be...."

~*Robert Browning,*
English poet and playwright
(1812-1889)

 **PRACTICE 4: Walk a Thousand Miles for the One You Love**

Write Your *Mile Steps* for Your Larger Relationship Goals

Review your *Big Picture Vision* (*Soulmate Statement*) for your desired relationship. From this broad picture, write out your major relationship goals (*Mile Steps*), such as marriage, children, values, and the activities you'd like to share (travel, archeology, rollerblading, bird watching, etc.). From these major goals, you will create your smaller *Mini Feats* steps. (There is a form in the back of the book, *The Mile Steps Spreadsheet*, that will help you chart this all out, or you can do this work in the *Blastation* software at www.InteractiveLifeCoach.com.)

Based on the *Mile Steps* above, your *Mini Feats* could be:

⭑ Take an archeology class.

⭑ Sign up for a bird-watching retreat.

⭑ Go to a bookstore and study the travel magazines.

⭑ Enjoy an afternoon of rollerblading with a friend.
  (From experience, I recommend learning how to use the brakes on those things before hitting the road with a date. Just picture an out-of-control rollerblader crashing into a hot dog stand in Manhattan's Central Park. It wasn't pretty.)

You are more apt to meet someone when you are partaking in an activity that you enjoy, rather than one you don't. So get busy. Your loved one is waiting! ✪

_____

_____

_____

_____

_____

_____

_____
_____
_____
_____
_____
_____
_____
_____
_____
_____
_____
_____
_____
_____
_____
_____
_____
_____
_____
_____
_____

"The best way to love
is to love like you've never been hurt."

~*Anonymous*

Blast Off! PRACTICE 5: What Do You Give Up in Relationships?

Do you enjoy reading but choose partners who prefer to watch television? Do you love boating but you choose partners who dislike the water? Are you a romantic but choose partners who think romance is "Hey Baby, what's for dinner?"

In the space below, make a list of the desires, needs, interests and philosophies that you tend to give up in relationships and then regret later. By making a list of the things that you feel are important, you can start to be aware of your choices and actions. Then you can create new intentions for a relationship that fits your ideal picture. ✪

_____

_____

_____

_____

_____

_____

_____

_____

_____

_____

_____

_____

_____

_____

_____

_____

_____

_____

_____

Blast Off! PRACTICE 6: Open Your Heart to Receive that *Supersonic* Love

Get into a quiet space or go to your *Inspiration Station.* Sit down and then take some deep breaths until you are feeling calm and relaxed. If soft music and candles help you get into the mood, add these to your environment.

Now when you inhale, visualize a golden light coming into your body from the crown of your head and see it flowing all the way down to your toes. Feel it as the warmth and the sparkling light nurtures all the organs and systems of your body.

After a few minutes, focus on your heart area. Now put your right hand over your heart and continue to inhale and exhale this golden light. Then as you inhale, only focus on your heart area and visualize a soft, pink, loving energy coming into your heart. Feel your heart opening fully and allowing this pink energy to fill it completely and fully with love.

If you have had pain in your heart due to loss or heartbreak, visualize the tears of your heart pouring out as the pain begins to release and subside. Fill any emotional wounds with this pink loving energy. See your wound healing as your heart is surrounded with love. Continue to inhale and exhale deeply.

After another minute or two, visualize the pink energy turning into red, passionate, vibrant energy that is continuing to fill up your ever-expanding, open heart. Now feel that love and passion spread from your heart to the rest of your body, up to your head and down through your torso and legs, and through to the bottom of your toes. Feel how wonderful, light, free and uplifting this love energy feels. Continue to experience the opening of your heart.

Now I want you to expand this loving energy inside your heart and the rest of your body out to the world and to the Universe. See it expanding for miles and miles. Oh, how lucky the world is to experience your love! Now feel the love coming right back into your heart and hold it there.

Your heart is now open and ready to receive love.

Repeat this exercise at least twice a week to continue healing and opening your heart so that you may receive all the love you deserve. ✪

"And the day came when the risk to remain tight in the bud was more painful than the risk it took to bloom."

~Anais Nin,
Cuban-French author known for her best-selling journals
(1903-1977)

Blast Off! PRACTICE 7: Set Your Intention with a Letter

Write your *Letter of Intention* and set a date for having your relationship. You don't have to send the letter to anyone for it to work, however, it is a good idea if you can. That will keep you accountable to your word, and you will not only receive the rewards of your own intention, you will also receive the power of your support team.

You can use the space below to work on your initial draft of the letter. ✪

_____

_____

_____

_____

_____

_____

_____

_____

_____

_____

_____

_____

_____

_____

_____

_____

_____

_____

_____

_____

_____

_____

Blast Off! PRACTICE 8: Bringing Your Soulmate into Your Space

Each morning and night, pull out your *Soulmate Statement* and read it out loud. Ask yourself if there is anything you are holding back or something that could be blocking your match from coming into your loving space.

★ Are you holding onto an unhealthy, going-nowhere relationship? Are you projecting self-doubt onto your intention?

★ Are you placing yourself into situations and places where you could meet new people, such as joining athletic activities groups, church groups, career networking groups, online dating services, alerting your friends that you are available, etc.?

Now see him or her coming to you and holding your hand as you do your daily activities. Come to know the feel of your soulmate's energy in your everyday life. See your Soulmate with you as if he or she is already here. See them coming to you, feel their presence, and believe it to be true. ✪

_____

_____

_____

_____

_____

_____

_____

_____

"Now join your hands,
and with your hands, your hearts."

*~William Shakespeare,
English poet, playwright and actor
(1564-1616)*

BLAST Off! Daily Launch Tools

1. Each morning, write your *Sun-Up Script* and *Rocket Words*.

2. Read your *Rocket Words* to yourself and out loud as often as possible during your day.

3. Create and perform a minimum of *Mini Feats* each day. (These are the smaller steps for moving toward your larger *Mile Step* goals and your *Big Picture Vision*.) For example, today's *Mini Feats* might be:

   - *Check out the online dating service my friends have been talking about. (Online dating doesn't have to provide the stereotypically bad experience you might have in your head. It's a great way to get to know a person who you may never have had the opportunity of meeting otherwise. In fact, you can use the service to invite "The One" into your life.)*

   - *Put all my ex-partners' photos in a box. Write a* Sun-Up Script *about releasing these relationships to the past to make room for the new and improved one. (If you do this* Mini Feat, *describe all the appreciation you feel for having experienced these past connections and any life lessons you may have learned.)*

   - *Read a book on feng shui to create an inviting area in my home for love to arrive.*

4. Choose one to two *Blast Off! Practices* from this chapter to do each day over the next week.

5. Fill out your *Weekly Flight Assessment Log* to review your week's progress toward realizing your *Supersonic Life*.

"Anyone can be passionate, but it takes real lovers to be silly."

~Rose Franken,
Novelist, playwright, short story writer
(1896-1988)

BLAST OFF! to New Heights for a Healthy Body and Mind

CHAPTER 6

> "Health is the greatest gift."
>
> ~Buddha,
> East Indian spiritual
> teacher and philosopher
> (563 BC - 483 BC)

By making simple changes or additions to your life, you can add *years* to your lifespan. You'll also feel so much better during this fantastic voyage you have been blessed with. To experience the best *Blast Off!* possible, keep your equipment healthy and countdown ready.

Three of the main things that most influence your health—stress, repressed emotions and your daily attitude—are among the subjects addressed in the practices ahead. You'll also find a practical energy work exercise (Practice 3). Chapter Six in the main book provides more details on these subjects and also discusses the importance of exercise and nutrition, as well as providing other beneficial health tips.

Blast Off! PRACTICE 1: Take Your Stress-O-Meter Reading
Down to Zero

By taking a look at what triggers your stress responses, you can become more aware and actively prepared to take care of yourself in these instances. At those times, you can use your "Stress-O-Meter" (your inner sense of stress rising) to create strength, empowerment and resilience, and eventually learn how to avoid the trigger altogether.

Make a list in the space below of all the stress triggers in your life—those people, events or instances that take you from a calm, peaceful state to a condition of stress, chaos, agitation, or an array of negative emotions. For example, your boss, your workload, finances, your mother-in-law, the barking dog, your neighbor....

_____

_____

_____

_____

_____

_____

_____

_____

_____

_____

_____

_____

_____

_____

_____

_____

_____

_____

Once you have acknowledged your stressors, the next step is to examine your part in creating the stress. Taking responsibility will remove you from victim mode and empower you into choice mode. I realize that it takes two to tango, but you are 50 percent of the equation. **Is there something you can do to shift the energy?**

Some possibilities include:

* Go to the gym on the way home from work to release your tension.

* Journal your feelings to make some space in your crowded, spinning mind.

* Start researching your dream career.

* Go to the theatre to see a comedy movie.

* Don't take your boss's ranting personally, since he most likely treats everyone that way.

I realize that it's not that easy to replace an overbearing mother-in-law, but you do have the power to decide how her actions and comments will affect you. If you can come up with some strategies to avoid, or initially reduce, your reaction to certain triggers prior to them happening, you'll be able to protect, deflect and shift your energy toward something much more positive. As a result, your healing energy will expand, rather than tense up and deflate.

Whenever you take action, even a small step (such as a *Mini Feat*) to alleviate stress or change a negative circumstance in your life, you will begin to feel better immediately. Your positive intention and action create a Universal momentum that will move you from feeling immobilized to back in the flow.

Now write down at least two possible strategies for each stressor in your life in the space provided.

For example: A difficult, complaining neighbor

* Try to talk to them and come to a compromise.

* If that doesn't work, before you completely lose your cool (which is pointless and will only create more stress), go deep within and conjure up some positive feelings and energy toward your neighbors, and then project this energy into the Universe.

_____
_____
_____
_____
_____
_____
_____
_____
_____
_____
_____
_____
_____
_____
_____
_____
_____
_____

Through the power of your intention, change will occur. ✪

"Smile at each other, smile at your wife,
smile at your husband, smile at your children,
smile at each other—it doesn't matter who it is—
and that will help you to grow up
in greater love for each other."

~Mother Teresa of Calcutta,
Humanitarian, advocate for the poor,
winner of a Nobel Peace Prize
(1910-1997)

Blast Off! PRACTICE 2: Breathe, Baby, Breathe

When you find yourself under stress, overwhelmed, running late, dealing with conflict or in an emotionally challenging situation, your body tenses up. You start gripping the steering wheel or gritting your teeth while thinking about what terrible thing is going to happen because you messed up big-time. Panic may even set in. Heart palpitations, tension headaches, and stomach upsets are a few of the physical reactions that you might have encountered in a stressful moment. If this is your state much of the time, you can see where chronic physical conditions could arise. **Your first line of defense is to breathe.**

Here is a breathing exercise you can do first thing in the morning, at your desk at work, in your car, or during just about any stressful moment. (You might want to find a private space.) Basically, you'll be breathing the stress right out of your mouth.

1. Inhale through your nose.

2. Take the breath deep into your lungs.

3. Feel your chest expand, then your abdomen. (If you're only feeling your chest expand, you are not breathing deeply enough. Breathing more deeply may take some practice to feel natural.)

4. As you exhale through your mouth, feel your abdomen flatten again.

5. Focus your mind on the sound of your own inhale and exhale, and on the vital life energy replenishing your body, mind and spirit.

Squeeze in five slow deep breaths at a peak stress moment and your heart rate will drop significantly. Then your mind will begin to calm so you can focus and make clearer decisions.

Practice 2 Bonus: Sighing. The big *uhhhhhaaaaaa* is the sound that comes after taking in a much needed breath at a weary moment. If you find yourself sighing frequently, most likely you're not breathing deeply on a regular basis. It can also be a sign that you are suppressing some emotion right under your chest cavity. (That is where the heart lies.)

Suppression is the opposite of expression. If you hold down your emotions on a regular basis, this can lead to an array of physical problems. *Blast Off! Practice 4* in this chapter will help you release your pent-up feelings. ✪

"This is life. Your life. Are you doing what you want?
Are you getting what you need?
Are you loving and caring for yourself?
...if not, why not?"

~Jennifer Louden,
Author of The Couple's Comfort Book

Blast Off! PRACTICE 3: Jin Shin Acutouch Treatment
(A Step-by-Step Self-Treatment)

Here's a treatment that you can give to yourself for immediate stress relief while sitting in your car or lying in bed at night. I use it all the time when I can't sleep, feel any physical pain, or just need to find calm in a stressful moment.

Jin Shin Balancing Exercise

1. Put your right hand on top of your head, palm down. Hold it there firmly until Step 6.

2. Put your left hand on your forehead. Hold it there for one minute.

3. Then place two fingers from your left hand under your nose so that the bottom finger rests at the top of your upper lip. Hold your fingers there for one minute.

4. Next, put your left hand on your chest for one minute.

5. Then position your left hand so that it covers your belly button and hold it there for one minute.

6. Then position your left hand so that it is on your pubic bone and continue to hold it there as you move your right hand under your tailbone.

7. Hold these last points for one minute.

You may already feel calmer by the time you get halfway through the exercise. Try it at bedtime and you may fall asleep before you finish. ✪

Blast Off! PRACTICE 4: What Emotional Energy
Are You Hoarding?

Emotions are a very healthy expression of energy, as long as they *are* expressed, not repressed. What unexpressed emotions are *you* carrying around in your body? As you lie in bed at night or walk about during the day, do you feel any pains or discomfort in your body? This exercise will help you get in touch with the emotions hidden behind the pain, and allow you to release them once and for all.

Go to your comfortable, private *Inspiration Station.* Close your eyes and use your breath to relax your body. Visualize any busy thoughts racing through your mind and then imagine them drifting from your brain off into the atmosphere. See your stressful thoughts or worries disappear into space.

★ Now that your mind is clear, focus on your physical body. Do you feel any pain, tension or discomfort?

★ Once you begin to connect with your pain, put your hand over the area that bothers you the most.

★ Now ask this pain what it's trying to express to you. If the pain could talk, what would it say? (You will be amazed at the insight and answers you receive.)

★ Start jotting down the answers that come to you during these sessions on the adjacent page. Don't analyze or judge your thoughts. Just keep your pen moving and don't stop to read what you have written. If you run out of space, you can begin to use your journal to record these notes.

★ Remember, suppressed emotions can hurt you and those around you. They create absolutely nothing positive for you or the world. Once you attain an awareness of the toxic energy that you have been carrying around, and then release and heal from the burden of these suppressed or pestering emotions, you will experience an awakening in your body that is expansive and freeing.

We don't realize how many emotions the body is holding on to, even if these feelings developed so long ago. Letting them go is like pulling up an anchor tying you to the past. To blast forward, you want nothing to hold you back any longer. ✪

_____
_____
_____
_____
_____
_____
_____
_____
_____
_____
_____
_____
_____
_____
_____

> "One of the common denominators for most of my non-well clients is an ongoing internal suppression of emotions, such as repressed grief, anger, resentment, regret or fear."
>
> ~Allison Maslan

Blast Off! PRACTICE 5: The Good News Diet

When we think or hear of uplifting news and events, our energy and mood immediately experience a joyful lift. If you were to focus on one positive happening at least three times a day, and at the same time, turned off and tuned out the negative news, your nervous system would feel calmer and your energy would begin to radiate.

Try this...

★ In the morning, at lunchtime and before bedtime, write down one word or sentence in this workbook that reflects some great news that has happened, recently or in the past, to you or someone you know. Or you can write something that you appreciate or are grateful for.

★ Be aware of the feelings that come up when you're focusing on this good thought. The more you draw your attention to the good news of life, the more you are putting that good-news intention into the Universe. And that positive intention will be reciprocated with even more positive energy.

Here's to your great news!

_____

_____

_____

_____

_____

_____

_____

_____

_____

_____

_____

_____

_____

_____

_____

_____

_____

_____

_____

_____

_____

_____

_____

_____

_____

_____

_____

_____

_____

For further reinforcement of healthful habits for life, see Chapter 6 in _Blast Off!_ ✪

"Dwelling on the negative
only contributes to its power."

_~Shirley MacLaine,
Award-winning actress, author of_
Dancing in the Light

BLAST Off! Daily Launch Tools

1. Each morning, write your *Sun-Up Script* and *Rocket Words*.

2. Read your *Rocket Words* to yourself and out loud as often as possible during your day.

3. Create and perform a minimum of *Mini Feats* each day. (These are the smaller steps for moving toward your larger *Mile Step* goals and your *Big Picture Vision*.) For example, today's *Mini Feats* might be:

- *Do Internet research on water filters to find the best way to purify my drinking water.*

- *Sign up for an ashtanga yoga class today.*

- *Find the closest grocery store that carries USDA Organic foods, and meats that are hormone and antibiotic free.*

4. Choose one to two *Blast Off! Practices* from this chapter to do each day over the next week.

5. Fill out your *Weekly Flight Assessment Log* to review your week's progress toward realizing your *Supersonic Life*.

"Love itself is a miraculous healing force."

~Bernie Siegel, M.D.,
Author of Love, Medicine & Miracles

CHAPTER 7

BLAST Off!
to Financial Freedom and Prosperity

> "When I chased after money, I never had enough. When I got my life on purpose and focused on giving of myself and everything that arrived into my life, then I was prosperous."
>
> ~*Wayne Dyer,*
> *Self-help author and lecturer*

After years of feeling stuck and unfulfilled, I officially hit a major impasse in my life path. I had no financial support, no inheritance looming, and zero in my savings account. The way I saw it, I had three choices: (1) cave in to the pressure, stay stuck, and allow life to continually overwhelm me; (2) resort to the same habitual ways of doing a job (or making money) that continually left me feeling emotionally flat and worn out; or (3) step out into the big unknown world, face my fears, and aim for a life with purpose.

To this day, I'm so thankful that I dug deep, gathered my courage, and opted for Door Number Three. Many people stay immobile and stick with Door Number One or Door Number Two because they feel that nothing is worth risking the security and stability of a lifestyle that they feel familiar and safe with, even if they're unhappy. I'm not criticizing this choice. Only you can determine the right path for you. There are realistic issues of responsibilities, the cost of living, education and retirement. I get it, because I was there too. But what I can say to help quell your fears is that when you're following your passion, the excitement and momentum you expel can create a financially rewarding outcome far above and beyond your survival consciousness. *The key is to move from survival thinking to abundance living.*

The practices in Chapter Seven start with identifying survival thoughts that may be running through your consciousness.

Blast Off! PRACTICE 1: The Energy of Your Survival Words

Your words are an unconscious expression of your life force. This is an inner game. You may be saying or thinking negative language that you're not even aware of. If you are thinking these thoughts, you are creating an energy frequency, and therefore, a negative reality around them. Let's take a look at all the ways you are experiencing and expressing survival thinking, which consists of repetitive thoughts and language concerning money that limits your financial growth.

Do any of these statements resonate with you?

* "Money never comes easily to me."

* "I never have enough."

* "I don't deserve to have money."

* "People will think I'm greedy if I have money."

* "Wanting money is a bad thing."

* "Money comes to others, but not to me."

* "I would love to travel, but I will never have that kind of money."

* "Money is dirty."

* "Whenever I try to make more money, I hit a dead-end."

* "Wealth only comes to rich people."

* "The economy is really terrible right now. It is a time of struggle."

* "I have a ton of bills coming up and no way to pay them."

* "I have to sacrifice important relationships and things in my life in order to receive money."

On the next page or in the *Blastation* software, make note of any of the above beliefs that you resonate with, and/or record your own additional negative beliefs and thoughts about money. This is your *Survival Thinking List.* ✪

_____

_____

_____

_____

_____

_____

_____

_____

_____

_____

_____

_____

_____

_____

_____

_____

_____

_____

_____

_____

_____

_____

_____

> "Whatever you do,
> don't give in to the voices inside your head
> that might be holding you back."
>
> ~*Patrick Phillips,* Author of
> How to Reprogram Yourself for Success

Blast Off! PRACTICE 2: Shift and Lift—Create Your Abundant Living Statements

By simply changing your thoughts and action from a negative to a positive—as you did with the flip-switching exercises in earlier chapters—the energy frequency in your body will shift upwards. This will help you to feel more confident and empowered.

Try this experiment. Say the words, *"I am stuck, broke and frustrated."* Repeat this statement five times.

★ How do you feel in your body as you repeat this phrase?

★ Do you feel your shoulders slump forward?

★ Do you feel heavier, as if there is a weight on your chest, shoulders or back?

★ Do you feel tired or anxious?

Now repeat this sentence five times, *"Money is flowing effortlessly and easily to me, and the Universe is taking care of all of my financial needs."*

★ Do you notice an energetic shift in your body?

★ Do you feel lighter and more uplifted with a sense that change is on the horizon?

Next, take the *Survival Thinking List* that you just compiled and flip-switch the sentences to positive *Abundant Living Statements* that have the polar opposite message and feel. (Do this on the next page or in the *Blastation* software.) The more specific you are about your needs and desires, the better.

For example:

"Wanting money is a bad thing."

Flip-switch it to:

"Money is a wonderful expression of energy."

"Money gives me a sense of freedom and choice."

"Money is a very positive asset because it gives me freedom."

"Money helps me to help others."

"The money I am receiving now will cover the cost of my tuition to culinary school."

Once you've completed your new list, start reading your *Abundant Living Statements* out loud each day. They'll be especially helpful when you feel any of the manipulative survival thinking energy beginning to play tricks with your brain again. Keep repeating your abundance phrases throughout the day, and you will begin to feel a shift in your energy, mood, spirit and motivation. Memorize the ones that seem to give you the biggest shift and lift, then incorporate them into your everyday language. ✪

_____

_____

_____

_____

_____

_____

_____

_____

_____

_____

_____

_____

"This is an abundant universe. There are no limits.
Just as the ocean doesn't care if you come to it
with a thimble, a cup, a bucket, or a tank car,
neither does the universe."

~*Jack Canfield*,
Author of The Success Principles

Blast Off! PRACTICE 3: Just the Fiscal Facts

You may feel that budget is a six-letter dirty word. However, a budget can help in many ways. It moves the anxiety about money out of your head and onto the paper. Once you know what your bottom line is (basically what you need to make in order to survive), then we have something to work with.

★ Look closely at and write down the total amount of monthly expenses that you listed in *Blast Off! Practice 5* of Chapter Four (the career chapter). I recommend averaging the past four months of expenses for a broader perspective. This is your *Blue Plate Special Number,* the amount of money that must be actualized to cover your expenses. Now you know that after these expenses are paid for this month (including any investment income and taxes), the rest is surplus. You can save the surplus, which I recommend, or spend it and make the world go round.

_____

_____

_____

_____

★ Now that you have your survival number, you can start to move beyond that. Way beyond that.

Knowing your bottom line will help you feel more in control of your finances so you can take action for growth and abundance. ✪

> "I have never been in a situation
> where having money made it worse."
>
> ~Woody Allen,
> *Film director, actor, comedian*

Blast Off! PRACTICE 4: Magnetize Your Money

Have you ever thought about someone you hadn't thought of in ages, and within the next day, they called you or sent you an e-mail? Have you talked to a friend about a venture or activity you wanted to be involved in (but didn't have the resources or contacts to get started), and all of a sudden, someone came along with all the answers you were looking for or they were the perfect person for you to talk with?

Your thoughts and words are powerful. You project them outwardly without even realizing it, and out of the blue, you receive. You can create the same response with money.

Set your financial intention through meditation on abundant thoughts and feelings, and watch the money roll in through unexpected checks and financial opportunities, inheritances, dream careers, windfalls—*you name it.*

★ **Practice with coins and work your way up to your treasure chest.** Focus your energy on finding fallen coins wherever you go. Start your day by projecting a powerful "feel good" desire and intention for finding coins. Meditate for sixty seconds each morning on this feeling, and see yourself finding these coins throughout your day. Keep your eyes open and make sure you have room in your pockets.

★ **Once you're comfortable and confident with receiving coins, shift your intention to dollars.** The money will appear on its own or in the way of fiscal opportunities. Once these opportunities appear, see how you feel about them intuitively. If your gut says "go," then take action. *Intention and action are the most powerful duo in the cosmos.*

★ **Write the amount you want to receive in your check register**, as if that is your actual bank balance. Just by writing that number down and telling yourself that the money is really there, you are setting your mental intention and projecting it outward. Your intention and action can change your make-believe vision into reality.

★ **Write a check for a major purchase that you plan to make in the next ninety days.** Whether it is for an upcoming vacation, a new computer, a house remodel or a business loan, write the check to "you" in the amount you need to have for this purchase, and put it in a safe place. As you write the check, visualize the amount you just wrote as if it were already in your bank account. Close your eyes and see yourself having the money to make your purchase. Repeat this visualization each day for forty-five seconds. Also, using a copy of the *Mini Feat Calendar* form from the back of this book, plan out your daily *Mini Feats* necessary to reach your goal. Then watch your dream unfold.

★ **Is there something you've been yearning to do, or to have?** Write a detailed short story (use the space below) with you as the main character involved in your activity, achieving your goal, or receiving your desire. Write about the experience as if it were happening now. Be very specific about how it looks, feels, how it turns out, what was said, and what you received from it. Read it out loud each day as you visualize and feel yourself performing your activity or receiving your desire.

_____

_____

_____

_____

_____

_____

_____

_____

_____

_____

_____

_____

_____

_____

_____

_____

_____

_____

_____

_____

_____

_____

_____

_____

_____

_____

_____

_____

_____

_____

_____

_____

_____

_____

_____

_____

It may take a week, a month or even bit longer to shift the energy from survival to abundance. Patience and persistence are required. You may have moments of feeling frustrated and doubtful of the pending positive changes. Acknowledge those feelings and then bring your thoughts and actions back on track. The reward for all of this intention and action will be well worth the wait. ✪

Blast Off! PRACTICE 5: Thank You, Bills, Thank You

If you're still obsessing about your bills twenty-four hours after you pay them, you are creating nothing but money-sucking energy around you. A positive shift needs to happen to keep your money from running down the drain.

To activate your cash flow, write down each monthly bill that you are paying in the blank space below. Think and feel appreciative thoughts in relation to these bills. Hold on to these uplifting feelings for at least one minute at time.

For example:

Bill	New Appreciative Thoughts
Water Bill	I so appreciate having clean, fresh water.
Babysitter	I am going to tip her because she takes great care of our kids.

By simply shifting the energy from feelings of loss or focusing on what you don't have, to thinking about abundance and the great things your money is contributing to while feeling appreciation, you will attract more of the same feelings of appreciation and abundance that you can bank on. ✪

★ **WORKBOOK BONUS** ★

The Seven Steps to Fiscal Wealth and Prosperity

Incorporate the following seven steps into your life and your money tree will begin to thrive.

1. Flip-switch your beliefs from negative to positive and know that money is abundantly available to you as you need it.

2. Set your mental intention by creating your financial *Big Picture Vision* and meditate on your financial goals.

3. Project your *Money Knowingness* outward through visually *feeling* your *Big Picture Vision* and financial goals. Do this at least 60 seconds each day.

4. Feel appreciation every time you give or receive money.

5. Take action steps every day, using your *Mini Feats* and *Mile Steps,* to move toward your positive intentions and your *Big Picture Vision.*

6. Think BIGGER than you ever thought possible and watch your wealth grow exponentially!

7. Expect to receive abundant wealth.

Make a copy of the Seven Steps and keep this list visible throughout your day. Post it on your bathroom mirror, near your computer screen, on your refrigerator, or someplace else where you frequently focus your attention. Read it morning and night. Utilizing the *Seven Steps of Fiscal Wealth and Prosperity* can help you to *Blast Off!* financially in a big way.

BLAST Off! Daily Launch Tools

1. Each morning, write your *Sun-Up Script* and *Rocket Words*.

2. Read your *Rocket Words* to yourself and out loud as often as possible during your day.

3. Create and perform a minimum of *Mini Feats* each day. (These are the smaller steps for moving toward your larger *Mile Step* goals and your *Big Picture Vision*.) For example, today's *Mini Feats* might be:

   ■ *Set up automatic payments from my bank account to pay my outstanding debts so that I don't have to focus any negative or worrisome energy as I pay them down.*

   ■ *Pull out my Gold and Silver Platters, and think about the actions that I'm taking to head in the direction of reaching these goals. (Try taking one action every day this week, e.g., make ten sales calls, raise your fees if applicable, etc.)*

   ■ *Look into developing a small business on the side. (Check out www.mysmallbiz.com for ideas.)*

4. Choose one to two *Blast Off! Practices* from this chapter to do each day over the next week.

5. Fill out your *Weekly Flight Assessment Log* to review your week's progress toward realizing your *Supersonic Life*.

"If your ship doesn't come in, swim out to it."

~Jonathan Winters,
Comic and actor

CHAPTER 8

BLAST Off!
to Adventure
and Amusement

> "It is a happy talent to know how to play."
>
> ~*Ralph Waldo Emerson, Essayist, poet and 19th century leader of the transcendental movement (1803-1882)*

What adventures and fun things are out there that you have always wanted to experience, but were afraid to try? Or maybe you feel like the time has never been just right. Well, people, the time will never be right, unless you choose to make it so. Today, right now, is the absolute perfect time to step out of your comfort zone and reach for your dreams.

This is your life, and you have complete power over your choices. You will know that you have found your bliss when you are wholly absorbed in that action, and in that moment, as if nothing else exists. Yes, it's time to get off the couch, or turn off the computer and step away from the office. Set your intention for more fun and adventure in your life, and then, as always, take action.

The practices in Chapter Eight will help you start moving along this delightful and invigorating path.

Blast Off! PRACTICE 1: Fun Finder

In the space below or in the *Blastation* software, make a list of fun stuff that you'd like to do. Then make a commitment to give some of the activities a try until you find a few that have that blast factor. (Try one for fun, see how it feels. If it's not a match, simply move on to the next.)

Enjoy the process. Experiment, experience... *Blast Off!* ✪

_____

_____

_____

_____

_____

_____

_____

_____

_____

_____

_____

_____

_____

_____

_____

_____

_____

_____

"To live is the rarest thing in the world.
Most people exist, that is all."

~Oscar Wilde,
Irish playwright, novelist, poet and
short-story writer
(1854-1900)

Blast Off! PRACTICE 2: What Are Your Top Three Funtastics?

From the list you created in Practice 1, choose three favorite activities that are most fulfilling to you. Note them below or in the *Blastation* software.

_____

_____

_____

If these three favorites are not already in your life on a regular basis, do whatever it takes to change that. For instance, make a point of regularly scheduling them into your calendar. These fun splurges will add leaps and bounds of joy to your daily experiences, improve your overall mood, and enhance your ability to maintain healthy relationships. They will help build self-confidence and relieve stress, while bringing you more into the present moment. ✪

> "Take time every day
> to do something silly."
>
> ~Philipa Walker

Blast Off! PRACTICE 3: The Smile Magnet

Nothing is more engaging than a smile or a laugh. What do you do when you walk by a stranger at the shopping mall or the bank? Do you barely say hello, then put your head down and keep walking? Or do you just look the other way pretending not to notice them?

We have become such a fearful, shut-off group of human beings that we miss out on so much magical interaction. One of the easiest ways to quickly connect with others and to manifest happiness is to look directly at a passerby and say, "Hi!" with a smile. Believe it or not, this alone can make someone's day, and the more happiness you create, the more uplifting energy you'll be surrounding yourself with. I challenge you to smile at as many strangers as you can for one week. See the amazing difference in your daily experience. You may just want to make this a permanent way of living! ✪

"Everyone smiles in the same language."

~*Anonymous*

Blast Off! PRACTICE 4: Destination Unknown

In the space below or in the *Blastation* software, list your favorite travel destinations and new places that you'd love to visit. Be bold, be daring, and explore the world. ✪

_____

_____

_____

_____

_____

_____

_____

_____

_____

_____

_____

_____

_____

_____

_____

_____

_____

"Stepping into another world will shift you out of your busy mind and into a soul-filled voyage."

~Allison Maslan

Blast Off! PRACTICE 5: It's Kid's Week

It's time to tap into that kid inside of you and embrace life with fun and curiosity. Pretend that you're looking through your eyes at age seven. Go through your week and experience as much as you can in your ordinary day from a childlike perspective. See how different every moment can feel with a shift in your approach and outlook. Write about this experience below, and as a continued practice in your *Sun-Up Scripts*. And remember, it's never too late to awaken those innocent childhood dreams. ✪

_____

_____

_____

_____

_____

_____

_____

_____

_____

_____

_____

_____

_____

_____

_____

_____

> "I think that's what life is all about actually—
> about children and flowers."
>
> ~Audrey Hepburn,
> *Film and stage actress*
> *(1929-1993)*

Blast Off! PRACTICE 6: **Put Your Muses to Work**

It's time to put your muses to work to inspire re-involvement in one of your past creative passions, or to motivate yourself to come up with a completely new one. How long has it been since you:

★ Played a musical instrument?

★ Wrote poetry?

★ Painted with finger paints or watercolors?

★ Tried ballroom dancing?

★ Took singing lessons?

★ Cooked for fun?

★ Worked in your garden?

In the space below, make a list now of all the creative endeavors you want to explore. Try a new one each week, and if you find ones that really click, make them part of your regular schedule.

_____

_____

_____

_____

_____

_____

_____

_____

_____

_____

Creative expressions can be practiced at any age. Try not to take them too seriously. Be in the moment and have fun. That is what matters most. You may be surprised to find how your spirit lifts, your energy improves, and your overall motivation increases. In fact, *your life may never be the same.* ✪

Blast Off! PRACTICE 7: Dream-Scaping

Here are some helpful tips for accessing, analyzing, and gaining insight from your dream life.

1. **Write down your dream as soon as you wake up**. If you wait, there's a good chance that the images will have already vanished. I believe our conscious mind is trying to protect us, so it forces these stories out of our head when we open up our eyes.

   It's helpful to keep a dream journal right by your bed. Write down as much detail as you can remember about your dream. Who was in it? What was said and done? What were you wearing? And most important, how were you feeling during the dream?

2. **Right after you have written down your dream, follow this up with writing about what you think the dream means to you.** Jot down any ideas, memories, hunches or thoughts. There is no right or wrong thought that arises or specific format in which to do this.

3. **Read back through the dream and see if you can come up with any additional detail**. What the people said in the dream, how the rooms were decorated, what the energy felt like in the dream. For instance, if you were watching an approaching tidal wave, what did it look like? Were you facing it alone? Was anyone there to support you? How were you feeling? What was the outcome? If you were alone, it could mean that you're feeling like you have to face overwhelming challenges all alone and you want some support. If you were rescuing someone, it could mean that the responsibilities in your life now (or in the past) feel overwhelming.

4. **Write down any other details and feelings you may have missed concerning the people or characters in your dreams.** See if these people or characters might relate to a particular aspect of your personality or life. Could they represent a hidden part of you, a deeply held desire, or a betrayal or a guilt that you're carrying around? What would you ask these people if you had the chance?

5. **What do you feel is the overall message or theme of your dream?** Is there anything you can learn from this dream? Is there a fear you would like to overcome? If it was peaceful, is this calming image something you can use in your meditation or as a creative muse? Is there an action that you need to take which your unconscious is trying to push you towards? Is there a gut-knowingness about something in your life that you're not facing? Is your dream calling you to have more fun, to find your purpose or passion, to spread your wings and fly?

6. **Draw, paint or collage your dream, if you are inspired to do so.** Often more insight and memory will be jogged through artistic expression. This is a way to make sense of the dream, release any negative emotions, and help yourself look at it objectively on paper for even deeper understanding.

   Use the space below to create a visual image of an important dream.

---

7. **Utilize stream-of-consciousness writing in your dream journal to release negative feelings in your dreams.** Several years ago, I kept having a recurring dream of an argument with someone I was very angry with, but had no way to express it to them in real life. Night after night, I would rehash this same argument. It was so frustrating and exhausting. One night after having this dream, I awoke and started writing my strong feelings wildly across the paper. I really let it all out. From that point on, I never had that dream again. The reason the dream kept coming up was because I needed to work through it and let it go. Let the paper know how you feel. *No holds barred.*

_____

_____

_____

_____

_____

_____

_____

_____

By learning to access, question and analyze your dream life, you open yourself up to a whole other part of your world—the one that exists from dusk until dawn. If you're having disturbing dreams that you cannot seem to shake, I recommend seeking out the counsel of a Jungian, art or sand-play therapist (see Resources in *Blast Off!*) to help unlock and hopefully shift them to more pleasant experiences.

Your adventure continues! ✪

> "You were born to fly,
> and in your dreams,
> you discover that the soul has wings."
>
> ~*Robert Moss,*
> *Author of* Dreamgates

Blast Off! PRACTICE 8: Your Giving List

In the space below, make a list of different charities or causes that you would like to give some of your time and energy towards. What causes or organizations have been calling to you? ✪

_____

_____

_____

_____

_____

_____

_____

_____

_____

_____

_____

_____

_____

_____

_____

_____

_____

_____

_____

_____

_____

"The love you keep is the love you give away."

~*Elbert Hubbard,*
Author, publisher, philosopher,
supporter of the arts
(1856-1915)

Blast Off! PRACTICE 9: Your Bucket List

In the 2007 movie called *The Bucket List,* Jack Nicholson and Morgan Freeman serendipitously share the experience of learning that their days on Earth are numbered because of their terminal illnesses. Morgan Freeman begins to write his bucket list, the things he wants to experience before he dies. Jack Nicholson encourages him to make the dreams come true and they proceed to leap from airplanes, eat caviar, explore the Great Wall of China by motorcycle, and express love to those who need to hear it.

Don't wait until your time in this world is limited. Live life today like there is no tomorrow.

In this exercise, make a list of all the things you want to do in this lifetime. Jot your ideas down in the space below, or input them into the *Blastation* software.

Next, do whatever it takes to experience each desire on your list. Mark it as accomplished when completed.

_____

_____

_____

_____

_____

_____

_____

_____

_____

_____

_____

_____

_____

_____

_____

_____

_____

_____

_____

_____

_____

_____

_____

_____

_____

_____

_____

_____

_____

_____

_____

_____

_____

_____

Now that you're packed with ideas for new adventures and amusements, don't procrastinate any longer. Start today. Break out of your box and begin to experience a more fully lived life. *Your Blast Off! life.* ✪

> "Life is so startling
> it leaves little time for anything else."
>
> ~*Emily Dickinson,*
> *19th century poet*
> *(1830-1886)*

BLAST Off! Daily Launch Tools

1. Each morning, write your *Sun-Up Script* and *Rocket Words*.

2. Read your *Rocket Words* to yourself and out loud as often as possible during your day.

3. Create and perform a minimum of *Mini Feats* each day. (These are the smaller steps for moving toward your larger *Mile Step* goals and your *Big Picture Vision*.) For example, today's *Mini Feats* might be:

- *Do research online for some travel destinations that I would like to explore.*
- *Call the local running club about joining.*
- *E-mail my friend Kris, who I haven't connected with for a while, and suggest we make a plan for lunch.*

4. Choose one to two *Blast Off! Practices* from this chapter to do each day over the next week.

5. Fill out your *Weekly Flight Assessment Log* to review your week's progress toward realizing your *Supersonic Life*.

"You grow up the day you have
your first real laugh at yourself."

~Ethel Barrymore,
Stage and screen actress
(1879-1959)

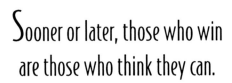

Sooner or later, those who win
are those who think they can.

~Richard Bach,
Author of Jonathan Livingston Seagull
and Illusions

Many Ways to Launch Your Dream Life

There are many more ways to launch your *Blast Off!* experience.

Visit www.MyBlastOff.com for information on:

★ Complimentary *Blast Off!* Newsletters full of valuable advice and tips.

★ Free download of the *Big Picture Vision Board* form, the *Mile Steps Spreadsheet,* the *Mini Feats Calendar,* and the *Weekly Flight Assessment Log.*

★ Audio version of *Blast Off! The Surefire Success Plan to Launch Your Dreams into Reality.*

★ E-book of *Blast Off! The Surefire Success Plan to Launch Your Dreams into Reality.*

★ *Blastation, the Interactive Life Coaching and Planning Software Program.*

To receive one-on-one support, contact Allison Maslan at Allison@ MyBlastOff.com or stop by www.MyBlastOff.com for information on her *Blast Off Life Coaching Program.*

To book Allison Maslan for a dynamic speaking engagement or for bulk sale pricing on any of the *Blast Off!* products, please e-mail our sales office at info@MyBlastOff.com, or call us at (888) 844-3550.

Big Picture Vision Board™

Describe your personal or professional vision in the first person
as if it is happening right this very moment.

Epic goal: _____

_____

_____

_____

_____

_____

_____

_____

_____

_____

_____

_____

_____

_____

_____

_____

_____

_____

_____

_____

_____

_____

_____

_____

Sample: Big Picture Vision Board™

Describe your personal or professional vision in the first person
as if it is happening right this very moment.

Epic goal: _Own my own clothing store in three years._

_____I am on the way to work at my clothing store called The Finer Things._
I actually love going to work now because it doesn't feel like a job.

_____I enjoy taking care of my clients and seeing them so happy when they_
find an outfit they love. Merchandising my window displays is fun and
challenging. It's an artistic outlet for me and I always do my best to draw
in clients. My business has been open a year now and last weekend we
had our biggest sales record to date! I am getting many return clients
and they are referring The Finer Things to their friends. I also
really love going to the marts and buying merchandise. It's always
exciting to see the next season's styles from the designers. I've
made some great friends in the industry, too. I am so thrilled and
proud of myself that I took a risk and went after my dream. My
business is already turning a profit and will double in sales in the
next few years. After five years, I plan to open my next location.

Mile Steps Spreadsheet™

Write your Mile Steps[SM] (the large steps that need to happen to reach your Big Picture Vision[SM]) on the top row of this spreadsheet. Vertically, under each Mile Step, write out all the Mini Feats[SM] that need to happen to make this Mile Step actualize. Then select the Mini Feats to input into your Mini Feat Calendar™. *Copyright © 2009 Allison Maslan. All Rights Reserved.*

Sample: Mile Steps Spreadsheet™

Write a Business Plan	Find location	Get Financing	Take a Business Class	Learn Buying/ Merchandising	Register Business	Set-up Accounting
Research business plans	Call area realtors	Call SBA for information	Research local colleges	Research area fashion colleges	File fictitious name	Research bookkeepers
Contact Score.org	Meet with realtors	Apply for credit line	Register- classes	Research online classes	Apply for resale license	Research tax accountants
Write business plan	Go visit locations	Research investors		Register for class	Open business bank account	Buy accounting software
	Research Craigslist	Ask Uncle Joey for $$				

Write your Mile Steps℠ (the large steps that need to happen to reach your Big Picture Vision℠) on the top row of this spreadsheet. Vertically, under each Mile Step, write out all the Mini Feats℠ that need to happen to make this Mile Step actualize. Then select the Mini Feats to input into your Mini Feat Calendar™. *Copyright © 2009 Allison Maslan. All Rights Reserved.*

Mini Feat Calendar™

Week from _____ **to** _____

	MiniFeat	Hour	MiniFeat	Hour	MiniFeat	Hour
Monday						
Tuesday						
Wednesday						
Thursday						
Friday						
Saturday						
Sunday						

Week from _____ **to** _____

	MiniFeat	Hour	MiniFeat	Hour	MiniFeat	Hour
Monday						
Tuesday						
Wednesday						
Thursday						
Friday						
Saturday						
Sunday						

Enter three valued activities each day in your Mini Feat Calendar™ that will move you toward your Big Picture Vision℠. Write the time of day you will be performing your Mini Feat activity so that you will be more committed to following through. Each Mini Feat needs to be a minimum of five minutes in length. You might plan the Mini Feats for the coming week on the weekend. Copyright © 2009 Allison Maslan. All Rights Reserved.

Sample: Mini Feat Calendar™

Week from *January 5, 2009*   **to** *January 11, 2009*

	MiniFeat	Hour	MiniFeat	Hour	MiniFeat	Hour
Monday	Research business classes	7:30 AM	Study business plan writing	12:30 PM	Research clothing stores	7:00 PM
Tuesday	Research business books	7:30 AM	Research financing	12:30 PM	Pick 5 stores to apply	8:00 PM
Wednesday	Research business class	7:30 AM	Research financing	12:30 PM	Fill out finance applications	4:30 PM
Thursday	Organize my office	11:00 AM	Study business plan writing	12:30 PM	Turn in finance applications	4:30 PM
Friday	Organize my office	11:00 AM	Research business coaches	7:00 PM	Study fashion magazines	8:00 PM
Saturday	Go hiking	8:00 AM	Meet Susan for lunch	noon	Finish office organizing	2:30 PM
Sunday	Read business books	9:30 AM	Start writing business plan	1:30 PM	Call Kathy to discuss my plan	4:00 PM

Enter three valued activities each day in your Mini Feat Calendar™ that will move you toward your Big Picture Vision℠. Write the time of day you will be performing your Mini Feat activity so that you will be more committed to following through. Each Mini Feat needs to be a minimum of five minutes in length. You might plan the Mini Feats for the coming week on the weekend. *Copyright © 2009 Allison Maslan. All Rights Reserved.*

Weekly Flight Assessment Log™

Date: _____

This evaluation is to assess the gains and roadblocks scattered along your new path. At the end of each week, fill out this assessment to evaluate your journey and your progress. Choose the keywords from below that resonate with you in each particular sector. Mark the applicable ranking in the space provided. Then briefly describe any gains or roadblocks for this past week. (Gains are any personal, emotional or tangible movement forward. Roadblocks are personal, mental or tangible challenges or detours.)

Gains & Roadblocks Keywords:

1. Stuck, trapped

2. Drained

3. Frustrated

4. Indecisive

5. Unmotivated

6. Bored

7. Exploring new options

8. Confused about what option to take

9. At a plateau, enjoyable but ready for more

10. So far so good, but time for the next level

11. Successful

12. Fulfilling

13. Inspiring and exciting

14. *Supersonic Wow!*

Career

Ranking _____

Gains _____

_____

Roadblocks _____

_____

Relationship

Ranking _____

Gains _____

_____

Roadblocks _____

_____

Health

Ranking _____

Gains _____

_____

Roadblocks _____

_____

Financial

Ranking _____

Gains _____

_____

Roadblocks _____

_____

Personal Fulfillment

Ranking _____

Gains _____

_____

Roadblocks _____

_____

Spiritual

Ranking _____

Gains _____

_____

Roadblocks _____

_____

Sample: Weekly Flight Assessment Log™

Date: _____ January 8, 2009 _____

This evaluation is to assess the gains and roadblocks scattered along your new path. At the end of each week, fill out this assessment to evaluate your journey and your progress. Choose the keywords from below that resonate with you in each particular sector. Mark the applicable ranking in the space provided. Then briefly describe any gains or roadblocks for this past week. (Gains are any personal, emotional or tangible movement forward. Roadblocks are personal, mental or tangible challenges or detours.)

Gains & Roadblocks Keywords:

1. Stuck, trapped

2. Drained

3. Frustrated

4. Indecisive

5. Unmotivated

6. Bored

7. Exploring new options

8. Confused about what option to take

9. At a plateau, enjoyable but ready for more

10. So far so good, but time for the next level

11. Successful

12. Fulfilling

13. Inspiring and exciting

14. *Supersonic Wow!*

Career

Ranking ___ 9 ___

Gains *I have reached the top level of management in my career.*
I learned so much and feel good about my accomplishment.

Roadblocks *I am missing the feeling of challenge and stimulation at work.*
I am feeling bored and ready to create a new path for myself.

Relationship

Ranking _____ 10 _____

Gains _I am putting more time and energy into my relationship. We've been_
having much more fun together and this has lightened my feelings of
stress in other parts of my life.

Roadblocks _I would like to create a lifestyle that allows us to take more time_
away together. I am feeling stuck on how to do this.

Health

Ranking _____ 9 _____

Gains _I made it to the gym four times this week. I felt tired but I was able to_
motivate my body to get there anyway. I now have so much more energy!

Roadblocks _I want to figure out a way to exercise during my lunch hour so_
that I have more time to do fun things after work.

Financial

Ranking _____ 8 _____

Gains _It looks like I will be receiving a nice bonus this year for all of my efforts!_

Roadblocks _I want to create a side business to supplement my income and_
to express more creativity and passion in my life. I need to find a coach to
help me do this.

Personal Fulfillment

Ranking _____ 6 _____

Gains _I am having more fun in my relationship._

Roadblocks _I am realizing that I have not tried any new activities in a long_
time. I am in need of some adventure.

Spiritual

Ranking _____ 3 _____

Gains _None_

Roadblocks _I planned to try some meditation or yoga and I have not been_
motivated enough to make it happen. I am going to create Mini Feats to
make both of these happen. I feel that they help me clear my head and feel
more connected to myself and others in all aspects of my life.

About the Author

Allison Maslan has been an entrepreneur for the past 25 years, and she has a vibrant and powerful array of successful businesses to her credit. Allison is an author, an international speaker, the originator and President of the *Blast Off! Life Coaching Program*, and the President of The Homeopathic Wellness Center where she practices as a Nationally Certified Homeopath and Licensed Holistic Health Practitioner. She is also the Founder of the Homeopathic Academy of Southern California, the largest and most comprehensive homeopathic certification academy in the United States.

In her twenties, Allison was co-founder and co-director of the Barali Group, a full-service advertising and public relations firm. Her client list included Supercuts, Allstate Insurance, Merrill Lynch, Charlotte Russe and MCI. She also co-developed, co-owned and sold a scuba diving certification program, Dive Pro San Diego, and a hair salon. And as a successful real estate investor, Allison manages several properties and coaches others to do the same. She is the author of many well-received articles in local, national and international publications. *Blast Off!* is her first book and others are being developed.

Allison Maslan has a doctorate in homeopathy from The British Institute of Homeopathy. She received her holistic health degree from Body Mind College in San Diego. Allison is certified as a homeopath through the Council for Homeopathic Certification, and she is registered with the North American Society of Homeopaths (NASH). She also served as the marketing director for NASH, which promotes homeopathy nationwide.

Through her years of working with clients on a one-on-one basis, Allison has come to understand how and why human beings create their own personal limits in different aspects of their lives, including in their relationships, personal joy, career, health, prosperity and spirituality. She developed the *Blast Off! Program* to help people learn to identify and release self-imposed roadblocks and create solution-oriented road maps to living abundant, richer and freer lives.

As a Master Life Coach and President of the *Blast Off! Life Coaching Program*, Allison utilizes her years of experience in building thriving businesses as well as healing, counseling and motivating thousands of individuals. Allison conducts one-on-one coaching consultations for personal and professional prosperity, and she can be reached at Allison@MyBlastOff.com and www.MyBlastOff.com.

The *Blast Off!* adventure continues. In addition to her *Blast Off! Life Coaching Program*, Allison has launched an online interactive coaching program called *Blastation*, available at www.InteractiveLifeCoach.com.

Allison Maslan lives in San Diego with her husband, Mike, three dogs, Daisy, Madison and Samson, and her cat, Miko. Her daughter Gabriella, who she raised largely as a single mom after her own life changes, is currently in college.

LaVergne, TN USA
31 August 2010
195257LV00001B/65/P